# unlocking the door

11  10  09  08  07  06  05    7  6  5  4  3  2  1

First published 2005 by Authentic Media,
9 Holdom Avenue, Bletchley, Milton Keynes MK1 1QR, UK
and 129 Mobilization Drive, Waynesboro, GA 30830-4575, USA
www.authenticmedia.co.uk

British Library Cataloguing in Publication Data
A catalogue record for this book is available from the British Library.

ISBN 1-85078-645-3

Cover Design and Typesetting by Adam Lees
Print Management by Adare Carwin
Printed and bound by J.H. Haynes & Co.Ltd., Sparkford

the door
unlocking

EVANGELISM IN THE REAL WORLD

Ruth Adams & Jan Harney

Authentic

ACTIVATE

# contents

# introduction

Before you begin, consider for a moment why you picked up this book. What attracted you to it? How much do you want to make a difference to the people around you? How important is it to see them wake up to the faith which drives your own life?

We believe that you are just the sort of person whom God chooses to build his kingdom. You may not think you are an evangelist; you might even worry about 'getting it wrong'. This book will convince you that the smallest efforts you make to connect with other people can make an impact beyond anything you expected or dreamt. God may surprise you with the results.

Activate exists to encourage everyone to be 'who they are, where they are – for God'. For those around your life, at work, rest or play, are those you are uniquely placed to influence for good. This might be simply by being you; as they watch your actions and reactions to the things you face. Or it might be through shared interests and opportunities. Or you could be proactive in harnessing the creative ways you could extend the friendship, by using something you read in these pages.

There are so many in Britain who have no concept of Christianity other than TV caricatures or negative news reports. They are certainly not asking the questions which will lead them to discover truth and eternity. They are, however, facing the same challenges and changes that you are and these common points can be the best starting place.

As you read on, let your imagination run free; let these pages inspire your own spin-offs.

## why do we need another evangelism resource?

Christians are busy people. Many of us are juggling work and family responsibilities and so often our leisure time is taken up with church-based activities or meetings. The result can be that we're in danger of being out of touch with those who have little interest in the church.

There are plenty of evangelistic resources available but most assume that Christians have a wide circle of contacts to invite to the various courses on offer. Yet our research shows that the majority of Christians – and church leaders – have few, if any, close friends outside their church circles. So, this is where this book will start, helping Christians build meaningful relationships with those in their 'circle of influence', whether this is in the workplace, the home, or through leisure activities.

# steps to christ

1. No awareness of God
2. Some awareness of God
3. Contact with Christians
4. Interest in Christ
5. Decide to investigate Jesus
6. Grasp the truth about Jesus
7. Acceptance of Christian truth
8. Understand the implications
9. Acceptance of implications
10. Commitment to Christ

We'll start at step 1 and, through a wide range of activities and ideas, show how every Christian can be salt and light, building up meaningful relationships with those around them.

# are we

*Every few hundred years throughout Western history a sharp transformation occurs. In a matter of decades society rearranges itself – its worldview, its basic values, its social and political structures, its art, its key institutions. Fifty years later a new world exists, and people born into that world cannot even imagine the world into which their grandparents were born. Our age is such a transformation.*
**Peter Drucker**[1]

Few would disagree with this statement if they consider the changes which have occurred in society over the past few decades. These changes have made it increasingly difficult for many Christians to relate their faith to the world around them and to express it to other people.

This graphic (see facing page[2]) is based on a photograph of a bridge in Honduras, South America and is taken from the *National Geographic* magazine. The little Lego-like structure in the front is actually a bridge that used to span the river. In 1998, Hurricane Mitch hit Honduras and one hundred inches of rain fell

# getting through?

in five days. In Honduras, that amount of rain is not unusual over six or twelve months, but in five days the effect was catastrophic, causing the river bed to move and devastating the landscape.

When change is gradual, we hardly notice it, but when it happens as quickly as it has over recent years, the effect can be more obvious.

Is this photograph an illustration of us as Christians? We stand firm no matter what happens around us, but have we ceased to be effective, a little like the bridge, which is now only a tourist attraction? The Japanese, who built the bridge, were delighted that it withstood the hurricane, but it's no longer fulfilling its purpose, because the river is somewhere else. The structures which we have in place may be strong and unmovable but are they fulfilling the purpose for which they were created? We need to look at some of the structures that we have in place in the Christian world. What was effective evangelism in the past may well be ineffective now because of the major changes in culture that we've seen over the last few decades.

The encounters of two young women, Emma, a journalist, and Joanna, a curate, illustrate this clearly.

In the course of her work as a reporter, Emma had to meet a photographer for an assignment at a well-known restaurant. They had never met before, but they got on well. Before long, discussion about glamour models had turned to religion and the church, and James was flabbergasted to discover that Emma, an attractive twenty-five-year-old, was a Christian. He confessed he had never before, in his forty-one years, met anyone who 'believed all that stuff.' Over a bottle of champagne their conversation continued until closing time. Emma works on what might be considered by some Christians to be a 'downmarket' Sunday newspaper, but in the course of her work she meets people who have often never spoken to a 'real' Christian before. Should this surprise us?

[1] Peter Drucker, *Managing for the future – the 1990s and beyond* (Middlesex: Penguin, 1992). [2] Photo, *National Geographic* magazine in November 1999. Taken by Vincent Musi

'The church is now an alien institution for the bulk of my generation, the iGeneration,' says Reverend Joanna Jepson, a curate in her twenties from Chester, who has received widespread publicity for her views on late abortions for 'minor' deformities. 'During time spent as a barmaid and youth worker among victims of drug abuse, I tried to get my mates to come to church with me, yet when one of them actually came I had to question the effectiveness of my plan. Scott was a punk who squatted in barns and ate speed and ice cream. He agreed to come to a service with me and did so for some weeks, until it was evident he was in danger of being turned into a middle-class Christian. He believed what he heard but the church didn't allow him to find language to express his growing spirituality. And I felt uneasy watching punk-boy head towards having to drain his hair of colour, lose the piercings and join the rows of homogenised, beige and navy Christians.

'Out of frustrations like this I, and others, have been provoked to go into ordained ministry in the hope of enabling those on the fringes to find a place of belonging. The church should not apologise for who we are and the truth that shapes our identity. But the language we use to express those things needs to speak to, rather than alienate, those who have grown up rarely crossing the threshold of the church.'

Like Emma and Joanna, if we want to help James and Scott and others like them find the reality of faith in Jesus, we need to spark conversations and friendships, and find new ways of living and communicating our faith in this changing world. People inside and outside the church are asking some important questions. Yet so often we are afraid to question what others have defined as non-negotiable.

Consider some of the questions and join the conversation.

What is the gospel?

Is it some information?

Is it an outline, laws, steps to help people go to heaven when they die? Is that all?

Does the gospel have something to say about experiencing God? Ecology? Power? The poor? Genetic engineering?

If the gospel is best described as good news, what should that news look like today?

How do we communicate the gospel today?

Is evangelism just learning the right phrases as they do in sales training? Or is it story-telling and hearing the stories of our friends and colleagues and our story as a follower of Jesus, together with God's story of creation, incarnation, the cross, resurrection and new creation?

# trying to reach

So often we get stuck in the mindset of wanting to bring people into our church buildings but this is not usually the best place to start. In the last census, for the first time there was an optional question about faith. Nearly 72 per cent of people who claimed allegiance to a faith ticked the box 'Christian' yet only a small percentage of them are sitting in church on a regular basis. Somehow we have got trapped into wanting to get people to come to church rather than to come to Christ.

Consider this quote from George Lings of the Church Army:

> To the unchurched, church is what some others do. It is noticed sadly, in their terms, not only as an alien and expensive building I wouldn't know what to do in, worse, it's occupied by people I wouldn't be seen dead with. To them church stands for internal bickering over issues no one else cares about, inconsistent lives that make claims in ridiculous words, led by people who don't know what they believe and are probably not to be trusted with other people's children.[3]

Many people's view of the Christian faith comes from what they hear on the news, see on the latest soap or watch on a TV programme. If they have never been inside a church, a fact of life for a huge percentage of the population, then television is the main source of information for them. Many, like James, the photographer, may never have even spoken to a 'real' Christian.

*The Richard and Judy Show* sent a reporter out onto the streets, as part of one of their programmes, to find out if people knew more about the signs of the zodiac or the Ten Commandments. A wide variety of age groups were questioned, and almost without fail, everyone could name the correct star sign which fell between two given dates, but hardly anyone could quote even one of the commandments correctly. This shows that we need to start where people are, not where we want them to be. Often people have far less understanding of the basics of the Christian faith – which we take for granted – than we realise. If we continue to stay in our safe ghettos and holy huddles, it's not surprising that the life in all its fullness which Jesus promised won't be conveyed to those outside the church.

[3] George Lings, *Encounters on the Edge – living proof – a new way of being church?* (The Sheffield Centre, 1999).

# your community

Community implies a level of acceptance and belonging, which we all need in order to establish some sense of status and self-worth. It has a part to play in the dynamic cycle of our very being. Community is about roots and identity. At its worst, it is suffocating and inhibiting. At its best, it brings comfort and shelter, a secure base from which to strike out and achieve our potential.

Do some research, as a group or an individual, and see if you can draw up a profile of the area in which you operate. It will take some time – but it'll be time well spent because it will give you a wider view of your community and some clues about ways to reach new people.

- How well do you know your 'patch'? Are you aware of the people who live in your area, or do you evaluate it by the people you know?

- List the places you visit in a typical week.

- What different types of people do you meet?

- What impression will they have of the Christian faith from their dealings with you?

- First make yourself a large map of your area by sticking together some pages from an A-Z. Mark on it key information, where you go to church, where your group members live and where you hold your events. Think about official boundaries; electoral ward or borough? Are there any natural boundaries; railway line, busy main road?

- Then study your map and identify the different 'pockets' of housing – large detached, pre-war semis, older terraced, executive housing and council estates. What about housing for special needs – sheltered housing for the elderly or disabled, flats and bed-sits for single people?

- Think about the people who live in these different areas and mark on the places where you think they might gather socially; the golf club, the Labour club, pubs, community centres, sports halls, bingo hall?

- Is there a great social divide?

- When is the community alive and full of people? When is it quiet?

- Where are the main areas of employment?

- What are the strengths and weaknesses of your community?

- How do you think God sees it?

- Can you find out how many people in your area are executives, single parents, unemployed, mums who go out to work, large families?

- What resources are there for children – such as play areas, parks, crèches, after school clubs?

- What is there for young people – youth clubs, coffee bars, sports facilities, discos?

- What is there for the 18-30s, young mums, elderly, divorced or bereaved people?

- Where are the gaps?

Try to be aware of what God is already doing in your area and then you can join in! Be bold when trying out new things in new areas. Praise God before, during and after everything you do, even when you think it was a flop. Then enjoy watching him honour your efforts.

# sources of information

* Local reference library
* Population census: try HMSO or the Internet
* Local authority ward profiles
* The local parish church – sometimes they have a parish audit, details are often held in diocesan offices (Board for Church and Society)
* Citizens Advice Bureau
* The front pages of your local Thomson telephone directory

# are we listening?

While the words 'religion' and 'church' might have negative connotations for some people, the word 'spirituality' is accepted by most of the population. Our society has never been more interested in 'spirituality' than it is today. The problem for us is that spiritual searchers aren't looking to Christians or the church for the answers to their questions, as they often don't feel we have anything to offer, but are turning to publications such as the increasingly popular monthly women's magazine *Spirit & Destiny*. Claiming to cater for the 'essential, inner, spiritual you' this magazine addresses people's desire for meaning by offering a whole range of alternative therapies.

This search for meaning was highlighted by a comment made by David Beckham: 'I want Brooklyn to be christened, but I don't know into what religion yet.'

Many Christians laugh at his lack of understanding, but David Coffey suggests that 'Our challenge as Christians is to find ways of relating to the bewildering spirituality of our times. People may appear superstitious but their questions are often a starting point that will lead them to a genuine encounter with Jesus Christ.'[4]

Diversity is God-given, yet we've narrowed things down and tend to treat everyone the same. For hundreds of years we've sent missionaries overseas and taken it for granted that they'd learn the language of the country they're going to. Yet, today in Britain there are many different cultural languages being spoken and we need a different language to reach each group of people. There's no one language that's better than another but if we're not speaking the same language as the people around us, they won't understand what we're talking about.

Some Christians, instead of demonstrating outside Mind, Body and Spirit fairs have now have begun to take stalls inside, creating opportunities to talk to spiritual searchers. They have offered prayer and ministry for healing and reported that they had a warm welcome from other stall-holders as well as positive conversations with browsers.

Sarah helped at a Journey Into Wholeness stand at a Nottinghamshire Mind, Body and Spirit fair.

> As the date for the Mind, Body and Spirit event came close I felt two different emotions. As I searched out and printed off Bible promises and prayers to make into give-away cards, and

---

[4] David Coffey, Address to the Baptist Assembly, 2002.

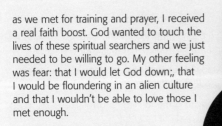

as we met for training and prayer, I received a real faith boost. God wanted to touch the lives of these spiritual searchers and we just needed to be willing to go. My other feeling was fear: that I would let God down;, that I would be floundering in an alien culture and that I wouldn't be able to love those I met enough.

I expected that we'd meet more spiritually hungry people in one weekend than in the rest of our lives, but there would be antagonism from the other stall-holders and the searchers. I knew we would be entering an alien culture with its own language and I was concerned that in speaking to people we would struggle to find points of contact. Above all I thought there would be bad spiritual 'vibes'.

What I found was acceptance. So many people, stall-holders and visitors responded when we 'confessed' to being Christians with 'It's great to see you here – it's about time the churches got involved.' We met lovely, caring people, desperate for

## 'I want Brooklyn to be christened, but I don't know into what religion yet.' DAVID BECKHAM

something to believe in, who we were able to talk to comfortably about God, our faith, prayer – the sort of things which usually make people look embarrassed and want to change the subject.

It wasn't always easy to work out which of the stalls was offering a therapy that was spiritual in its approach and which were purely physical, but the make up of the stalls was about one third merchandise, one third holistic therapy and one third clairvoyants and witchcraft. One very sad thing was the number of people we met from a Christian or church background who had been hurt or disappointed by the church and had turned elsewhere to have their spiritual needs met. They needed very little prompting to tell their stories and talk about their needs and the problems they faced. If we know people who are searching in this way, visiting clairvoyants or reading their horoscope regularly, then (rather than be disapproving) we might look upon it as an opportunity to engage them in conversation and to find out what it is they are looking for.

Returning to church, Sarah wrote the following words:

Too often we've been happy to come to Him
for blessing and not been prepared to go out and bless

We've been happy to come to Him for hope and not been prepared to go out and offer hope

We've been happy to come to Him for comfort and not been prepared to go out and offer comfort

We've been happy to come to Him for healing and not been prepared to go out and offer healing, to a hurting, desperate world, and so the world has looked elsewhere.

○ **How willing are we to engage with the spiritual searchers who are almost certainly living and working around us?**

○ **Do we know how to have meaningful conversations or are we only programmed to give standard Christian answers?**

○ **Can we see opportunities in our everyday encounters?**

We need to listen before we speak. We have lots of answers to questions that no one is asking, questions that don't connect with people. Many evangelism courses consider questions like 'What is God like?' and 'What is sin?' Yet most people aren't asking those questions. They're asking, 'How do I live with a diagnosis of cancer?'; 'How can I hold my marriage together?'; 'How do I cope with my kids?' or 'How can we survive redundancy?' When we come alongside people and help them as they ask these questions, we may find that later we have the opportunity to answer some of the deeper theological questions, which many evangelistic courses deal with.

A message can be one hundred per cent true and one hundred per cent irrelevant. There's nothing wrong with the message we have, and often those around us haven't rejected the message, it's just that it doesn't connect with them because we don't listen to their concerns and questions, affirm them and meet them at their point of need as Jesus did. There is no magic formula for successful evangelism but integrity and common sense are vital ingredients, and we may need to throw stuff out that we've inherited from the past.

# modern britain
## – ancient athens reborn

We might not feel particularly at ease in areas which are outside our comfort zone, but that doesn't mean we should avoid them at all costs. Canon John Young says, 'Modern Britain resembles ancient Athens – plus mobile phones and parking problems, of course. Does this present an opportunity for the Gospel? Clearly it does, but only if modern Christians and the churches to which they belong are prepared to engage with our secular and superstitious culture with energy, imagination and sensitivity. Over to you. And over to me.'[5]

In Acts 17 we find the apostle Paul in Athens. Paul wasn't very happy with the mishmash of spirituality that he encountered there but he was able to speak into the culture and use their altar to the unknown god to make Jesus known. Maybe a parallel today would be a Mind, Body and Spirit exhibition. Paul wasn't at ease in Athens but he expected to find God there. He was prepared to trust God even on what he felt was dangerous territory.

Do we believe that God is at work in the most unlikely places in his world? Some Christians feel that God is doing more outside the church today than he is inside. What do you think? What is God doing? Where is he working? How can we get alongside his work rather than insisting that God comes alongside what we're doing?

Paul was alone in Athens, he had no support group. He listened to and watched what was going on as he walked the streets and talked to anyone who happened to come along. He got to know some of the intellectuals pretty well through these conversations. Some of them dismissed him with sarcasm, but others listened and said 'We want to hear you again on this subject.' (Acts 17:32). Paul affirmed people's starting points. He didn't shake his head in Athens and say, 'We'll need to clear the shelves before we start.' He asked, 'What are the pegs to hang the message on?' He sees the altar to the unknown god and uses this as a starting point to share the gospel. What are the equivalents in the lives of the people we know?

Bruce Stanley, the designer of the rejesus website (a great resource for friends who are considering the Christian faith – www.rejesus.co.uk) gives one example of how this can work.

[5] John Young, *Christian Herald*

This year was my mother's sixtieth birthday party. She had a big gathering of friends for a weekend of circle dancing, story-telling and music with me there as the son who's into spirituality and stuff. I love rites of passage and ritual and I wanted to create a service to mark the occasion. If there can be dream catchers, animal spirit guides and crystals at the party then I'm not going to leave the real thing outside. So with some minor tweaks to language, I used some fantastic prayers and responses from the Northumbria Celtic Daily Prayer book. I love taking God out to where people are and sidestepping hang-ups about religion that bore me senseless.

One woman who runs new-age retreats told me afterwards that it was a privilege to be there and she only wishes she could have something similar for her birthday. When you taste the real thing you know the difference.

To most people, Jesus is a historical figure, not someone who is present. I believe that asking questions is more useful than telling people stuff. I am nothing extraordinary; I don't feel I have all the answers and I certainly don't always live life as some shining example of Jesus. Yet at an unconscious level I have come to believe in being real, vulnerable, reflective, genuine and bold – all learned the hard way. And lastly and most importantly I need and like making friends (with or without my faith) and investing in those I already have. And that is it! Be available and have some fun out there.

So how do we communicate our message to people? Let's begin by looking at how Jesus did it in Luke 10:25-37. The rich young ruler asked Jesus, 'What must I do to inherit eternal life?' How would you answer that question if someone asked you this today?

Let's see how Jesus responded. He asked a question and then told a story. Maybe that's not the way we would have answered, but much of Jesus ministry was taken up with asking questions and then telling stories. Is there a lesson for us here?

Read the story in Luke 10:25-37 and then consider the following questions.

○ What evidence is there in our society that people are interested in eternal life?

○ The man in the story was robbed and left for dead. What have the people round you been robbed of? (e.g. freedom, family, job, health – the list is endless)

○ Who would the priest and Levite represent today?

○ Why didn't they stop and help the injured man? Have those we know good reason to view us in the same way?

○ The Samaritan *'came where the man was'*. Where are people around us today – geographically, emotionally, socially and psychologically?

○ In order to help the man the Samaritan had to get off his donkey. What are some of the *'donkeys'* we may need to leave?

○ It cost the Samaritan both in time and money to help the man. What sacrifices are we prepared to make in order to come alongside those around us?

○ Which person in the story do you most relate to?

# how did Jesus

If we look at the many ways and circumstances that Jesus used to reach out to people we might get some clues. If we look at the different types of evangelism Jesus modelled we can see that there was no set formula. Jesus didn't sit in the synagogue waiting for people to come in: he got out and about wherever people were, healing and story-telling. We need to follow his example and talk to people about their work, their hobbies, their concerns, and the things that interest them or are relevant to their lives. These will ultimately be the pegs on which we most effectively hang our message. We start where people are and gradually find ways to create a forum for further discussion.

Jesus was often to be found eating with people that others shunned. In Mark 14, he's at the house of Simon the Leper, having perfume poured on his feet and wiped away with a woman's hair. Respectable women always had their hair fastened up! At other times he's to be found eating with tax collectors. Either way he enjoys relaxing, eating and chatting with people. Jesus often encouraged others to eat in his company. It's usually where the best conversations take place. When Jamie Oliver produced his little cookery book for *Comic Relief* he suggested throwing dinner parties to raise money for charity: meeting for a meal is an excellent way to relax with friends.

# reach his world?

If we follow Jesus' example we're likely to be successful in making friends and influencing people, although it won't always be easy. Jesus talked to the people about vineyards, sheep, farming and fishing, the things that they were actively occupied with. We rather miss the point when we do this in inner-city Manchester today.

Jesus was often criticised for hanging out with the wrong sort of people. Social outcasts of all varieties were drawn to him. The first reference on the on the list on the next page (Luke 5) tells the story of Jesus calling Levi to follow him. Tax collectors were excluded from the synagogue; they weren't allowed to be judges or witnesses and their disgrace extended to their family. Jesus was

launching a new style of inclusive ministry here. Is this the attitude we have as Christians? It is interesting to consider what Jesus did with Levi once he'd accepted his call. He didn't take him to the synagogue to begin a nurture group but suggested they went to Levi's house where Jesus could meet his friends, described as notorious sinners.

The reference from John 4 is the story of the woman at the well. Much has been written about this encounter but it's interesting to note that Jesus actually said very little – he didn't bombard her with information or appear to judge her harshly but just answered the questions she asked him. How much listening and asking

questions do we do, in comparison to how much we talk at people? Matthew 19:16-22 is the story of the rich young ruler. What did Jesus talk to him about? Money. And the reference from John 3 finds Jesus debating theology with Nicodemus, an expert in the subject. 'You must be born again.' How much has that phrase been abused by hitting lots of confused 'non-theologians' over the head with it? Nicodemus was a member of the Jewish ruling council who went secretly, at the dead of night, to Jesus and asked him some questions. He seemed to be sincerely pondering and searching. And because he was a theologian of the time, Jesus presented him with some deep theological thinking.
He was meeting Nicodemus 'where he was', speaking to him in appropriately pitched language, just as he spoke to fishermen about fishing, rich people about money and the woman at the well about water.

Jesus was an expert at talking to people about the things they were interested in. Today he'd probably talk to them about work, TV, gardening, DIY, fashion and beauty as well as current issues, both personal and national. Jesus set Nicodemus thinking and helped him on his journey; there was no 'in-your-face' pressure for him to make a decision for Christ and sign a form. He let him go away to think it through.

In John 7 we see a bolder Nicodemus publicly arguing for fair treatment of Jesus and pointing out the inconsistency of the Pharisees. They were demanding that people kept the law but were trying to sidestep it themselves. So Nicodemus is insisting on integrity in the midst of this highly irregular proceeding. He makes enough of a stand for his colleagues to challenge him about his allegiance to Jesus.

And note the Bible reference for the conversation with this theologian. Look what it contains, John 3:16, 'For God so loved the world...' This is our gold nugget and it was in Nicodemus that Jesus planted this gold. In the account of Jesus' burial in John 19 we see Nicodemus helping Joseph of Aramethea to prepare Jesus' body for burial. It's just hours before the Sabbath, and touching a dead body would have made him ritually unclean for seven days, requiring purification twice. How would he have explained that away to his peers on the eve of Passover, a major Jewish festival? John writes that Nicodemus brought along a mixture of myrrh and aloes, about seventy-five pounds. This was a very large amount, about two large sackfuls. That amount would really only be appropriate in royal burials. It seems as if Nicodemus was making an important statement.

So although we don't see Nicodemus listed among the names of the believers as the church grows, he's obviously making progress on his own journey, in his own way. Who knows what impact he was able to make on the lives of other Jews, quietly and studiously? Was he making use of where God had put him rather than feeling the need to leap into a new life? We don't need to know. Nor do we need to pin down the people in whom we're sowing seeds. We can just relax with them, be there for them, try and answer their questions and encourage them. But we don't need to check them for progress – unless we're desperate to collect scalps or count heads.

## how Jesus reached his world

| | |
|---|---|
| Luke 5:27-31 | **Work Colleague** |
| Mark 2:1-11 | **Home Evangelism** |
| John 5:1-14 | **Individual** |
| Mark 1:35-45 | **Village Evangelism** |
| Matt 15:29-38 | **Big Event** |
| John 4:1-42 | **Social Outcast** |
| Matt 9:1-8 | **Friendship** |
| John 8:1-11 | **City Centre** |
| Luke 19:1-9 | **Opportunity/Home** |
| Luke 13:10-17 | **Sabbath Day** |
| Luke 14:16-23 | **Banquet** |
| Luke 7:36-50 | **Dinner Party** |
| Luke 15 | **Lost and lonely** |
| Luke 10:25-3 | **Good neighbour** |
| Luke 8:1-15 | **Outdoor** |
| John 3:1-21 | **Debate** |
| Matt 19:16-30 | **Topical** |

what is our
masterplan?

When a house is being built there is very little to see for weeks because the foundations are being laid. Psalm 127 says 'Unless the Lord builds the house its builders labour in vain'. As Christians, we acknowledge that everything we do must be wrapped in prayer. We cannot build on shaky ground but only on the Rock that is Jesus. So, what guidelines has Jesus given us for evangelism?

In his book *Prayer Evangelism*, Ed Silvoso[6] says that there is only one occasion in the Gospels where Jesus spells out an evangelistic method: Luke 10:5,8,9.

'When you enter a house, first say, "Peace to this house." 'When you enter a town and are welcomed, eat what is set before you. Heal the sick that are there and tell them, "The kingdom of God is near you."'

1. Speak peace to them
2. Spend time with them
3. Take care of their needs
4. Proclaim the good news

This four-step method proved so successful that soon after Jesus taught it to his disciples, multitudes came to believe in Jesus. We tend to reverse the order and begin with the last step – and it doesn't work.

In the book, Ed Silvoso talks about our circle of influence and it's important that each of us identify who this group is, in our lives, at any given time. It may be those who live in the homes around ours, those we work with, or the other parents at the school gate. One woman realised that the other women she was receiving

chemotherapy with for breast cancer, were her circle of influence at that point in her life. Take a few minutes to think about who might be in your circle of influence.

O Consider those who are part of your family, work colleagues, neighbours and contacts through leisure activities.

O What are their needs, expectations and interests?

We'll refer to the circle of influence as neighbours here, but adapt that word for those you have now identified as being in your circle.

Sinners loved to hang around Jesus, because there was something about him that drew others to him. Our neighbours should feel the same way about us, as we are his representatives on earth (Lk. 10:16). Yet, so often we are decidedly un-Christlike in our interaction with those within our circle of influence. We barely put up with them and make it painfully clear that we can't wait for them to change and become more like us. This is a destructive attitude unworthy of Christ and his kingdom. We must spend time with our neighbours not to patronise or proselytise but to receive from them. Jesus' method calls for two-way fellowship with an emphasis on receiving rather than giving.

Once we have broken the ice with our neighbours, we don't need to rush to share the gospel with them. Spending time is the next step. It provides an opportunity to show unconditional acceptance by welcoming them just the way they are instead of the way we want them to be. Jesus instructs us to *receive* from them. 'Stay in that house, eating and drinking whatever they give you' (Lk. 10:7). It's important to allow others to do things for us as well.

[6] Ed Silvoso, *Prayer Evangelism* (California: Regal, 2000).

*we are not told to bring our neighbours into the kingdom; we are to take the kingdom to them.* **ED SILVOSO**

Blessing opens the door to fellowship and fellowship eventually leads to the third step, an opportunity to meet their felt needs. This will only happen as they trust us enough to disclose those needs. We may then be able to say 'I've been praying for you, let me pray about this too.' Often unbelievers understand prayer better than we do and they rarely refuse an offer of being prayed for.

We are not told to bring our neighbours into the kingdom; we are to take the kingdom to them. This is like driving through the desert in an air-conditioned truck stocked with cold drinks. When you spot a weary pedestrian lost on a lonely road on a hot summer day, if you pull up next to him, you don't have to beg him to come on board. All you need do is pull over near to him and open the door. Why should people believe that we, complete strangers, are going to heaven and that they are going to hell? Why should they believe that the Bible is the word of God? To them it's no different from the book of Mormon, or the sayings of Buddha or Mao. What credibility do we have to cause them to believe anything we say? For credibility to develop, a process is necessary and this is where prayer evangelism comes in. Caring for people is at the heart of Jesus' strategy.

How much do we care for those within our circle of influence? In his book, Ed Silvoso admits his attitude towards his neighbours needed changing before he could put the principles of Jesus into action where he lived.

> I became aware of my own belligerence towards the lost the first time I tried to implement the Luke 10 strategy in our neighbourhood. Instead of claiming the promises of God to deal with the problems I saw in my neighbours' lives, I told God about everything that was wrong with these people.
>
> I talked to him in disgust about the unmarried mother and how she had to change because she was such a bad example to my daughters. I demanded that he do something about the couple who kept us awake at night with their arguing and fighting. I complained about the depressive neighbour whose garden was a disgrace and brought down the property values in our area. And of course I did not forget about the teenager on drugs. I made it perfectly clear to the Lord what a detriment this young man was to our neighbourhood.
>
> All of a sudden I sensed God saying, 'Ed, I am so glad you've not witnessed to any of these yet.' Surprised I asked, 'Lord, why

is that?' His reply was very sobering: 'Because I don't want your neighbours to know that you and I are related. I hurt when they hurt. I reach out to them. I constantly extend grace to them. I am the God who causes the sun to rise over the righteous and unrighteous alike. I love them. But you don't. You resent them. Rather than being an advocate for them, a lawyer for the defence, you are instead a witness for the prosecution... if not the prosecutor himself.' Then he rebuked me saying, 'Unless you love them, I cannot trust you with their lives.'

So there is a need to take this blueprint for evangelism in the gospels seriously. Each of the four points rolls on to the next. When you are friendly to someone, you begin to get close. When you spend time with someone you get to know what their needs are. Then you can offer to pray with them. Very few people say 'No.' Once you've prayed for someone the way is open for relaxed conversation. Talk about everyday things that surround you – like Jesus did. Just be yourself – we call it using 'what you've got in the house'. And eventually you'll get the opportunity to talk about your faith in a gentle way that prompts interest and questions.

# gender roles
## – are they blurring?

A glance along any newsagent's shelves will reveal a host of magazines catering for a huge variety of tastes. Nothing new about that, but the significant difference today is the increase in the number of magazines for men. A closer look at some of these publications will show a close resemblance between the issues covered in magazines for men and for women. Almost every magazine for women includes articles on health, sex, relationships, and lifestyle, and the magazines for men are increasingly covering the same issues month by month.

Nick Pollard, founder of Damaris (www.damaris.org) writes this about gender roles.

'I'm a man, but I'm not really sure what that means.' This was the start of a very interesting conversation about identity, value and the message of the Bible with a friend of mine. It probably could have been with almost any of my male friends or acquaintances, since throughout our culture there seems to be a general uncertainty about what it means to be male.

There are those with a very definite answer. Colin Wolfendon and Nick Bagrie, for example, are homosexual designers and the eponymous *Fairy Godfathers* of the recent Channel 4 series. In these programmes we watch them move in to live with a variety of men and work on their grooming, dress sense, interior design and cuisine – until they have created what they call 'caring, sharing, new men'. Is that what we need? To become, in their words, 'more gay'?

On the other hand, journalist and commentator Melanie Phillips presents a rather different view. In her book *The Sex Change Society*[7] she argues that there has been 'a disturbing attempt to feminise the state, to reverse the roles of men and women and to run masculinity out of town altogether.' In this book and her more recent articles, she seeks to show that this attempted 'neutering of the male' doesn't just lead to feelings of guilt and uncertainty amongst men, but also to injustice in the legal system and in the educational system.

Whatever we think of Melanie's arguments or Colin and Nick's makeovers, it certainly is possible to trace a significant shift in the portrayal of men and women in the media over the last few decades – and to consider the effect that this has had upon men today.

[7] Melanie Phillips, **The Sex Change Society** (The Social Market Foundation, 1999).

Twenty years ago men and women were largely (with some exceptions) portrayed according to their traditional stereotypes. This was a time in which Arnold Schwarzenegger and Sylvester Stallone played rough, tough, fighting heroes. Now the action hero's purpose seems to be shifting from physical to relational. One can see examples of this in films such as *The Patriot* (2000) and *Master and Commander* (2003). In *The Patriot*, Mel Gibson plays a lone parent who is reluctant to join the American War of Independence – he would rather be at home with his family. In *Master and Commander*, Russell Crowe plays a naval captain during the Napoleonic wars. He is a strong leader who can command his ship and win battles against all the odds. But he is also a complex person who loves to play classical music and who has a very deep friendship with another man, the ship's doctor. As much as this is a traditional action/adventure film, it is also a modern study of male friendship.

Meanwhile, what has been happening to women? Here we can trace the other side of the coin – as women increasingly play roles with aspects that were traditionally male. Take, for example, the trilogy of *Matrix* films. In these, Trinity is far from a helpless female – she can shoot and fight better than most of the men. Indeed, by the third film many of the heroic fighters are women like Niobe – she flies a hovercraft back to the battle in Zion on a route that the men consider to be impossible. Zee and other women are already fighting at the front line on equal terms with the men.

Perhaps this change is most evident in those series that span the last few decades. Think of the Bond films for example. They always contain a Bond-Girl – but the way in which these are portrayed has changed. In the early films they tended to be helpless victims with a habit of making things worse by accidentally knocking levers with their bottoms. Compare that with Halle Berry in the film, *Die Another Day* (2002). She is beautiful, but also strong, confident and powerful. Similarly, in the recent feature-length pilot for a new series of *Battlestar Galactica*, the character of Starbuck has changed from a man to a woman. Starbuck was a dangerous, risk-taking, gambling, cigar-smoking man. Now the character is female, yet she behaves in exactly the same way – which includes the cigars.

What is going on here?

Is this recognition that traditional male/female stereotypes don't describe real people?

Is this an acknowledgement that all of us, male and female, have the capacity to be strong, powerful and authoritative – as well as warm, soft and sensitive? Or is this an example of the way in which our society is becoming feminised, and men are becoming neutered?

Whatever is happening, there is no doubt that many men are struggling to work out what it means to be a man. Perhaps now, more than ever, men are open to thinking about questions of value and identity – about spiritual and moral questions.[8]

[8] Taken from Nick Pollard's 'Gender Roles' article, first published in **Idea** magazine. Used by permission. See www.culturewatch.org.

does anyone understand men?

# 'now apparently, the divide between the sexes is getting smaller'

'Why can't a woman be more like a man?' Rex Harrison asked in the role of the misogynist Professor Higgins in the film *My Fair Lady*. But now, apparently, the divide between the sexes is getting smaller. The so-called 'New Man', celebrated by popular women's magazines, is a more sensitive character, more able to acknowledge emotions and more likely to take a share in the domestic chores and the rearing of children.

So, just how alike are men and women in other areas of their lives? According to *The Guardian* newspaper, an independent poll was conducted recently to assess this question. Participants completed a confidential questionnaire that was then placed in a sealed envelope. Interviews were conducted across the country and the results have been weighted to reflect the demographic profile of all adults. Regarding the 'New Man' emotional profile – only 1 in 10 felt that the movement towards emotional honesty has gone too far and this group was largely made up of older men. There is certainly no evidence that women wish men to curb their emotional outpourings or that they hanker for the return of a more traditional stoicism.

When asked: 'Do you think that the differences between men and women are becoming less pronounced over time?',

the answers were very similar, Yes: 68 per cent (Men) 71 per cent (Women); No: 32 per cent (Men) 29 per cent (Women).

When asked how interested they were in their appearance, there was very little difference in the answers from males and females questioned. Answers ranged from 'Not interested' to 'Extremely interested' and 21 per cent of males were in the top bracket, with 22 per cent in the next level of 'Very interested'. The conclusion was that a large proportion of UK men are extremely interested in their physical appearance and are happy to admit it. In fact, men are only slightly less interested in their appearance than women.

The same similarity was found between the character traits of men and women, and what they each found attractive in the other.

The message has clearly permeated male skulls that a good sense of humour can excuse a multitude of sins. Men believe that humour is the trait most likely to attract women, and women agree. Indeed, what is interesting about the poll results is the extent to which men are aware of what attracts women, possibly thanks to years of idly flicking through women's magazines.[9]

Those who feel that the differences between the genders are

[9] Poll analysis by Jim Mann, *Observer* Research Department.

becoming less pronounced will be interested that the characteristics women find attractive in men are very similar to those that men find attractive in women. Men are most attracted to a woman with a good sense of humour, a trait that equals even appearance and looks in terms of male priorities.

To the question 'Are you currently, or have you ever been, a member of a gym?' the answers were almost identical again:

Yes, currently: 22 per cent (Men) 24 per cent (Women)
Yes, used to be: 22 per cent (Men) 21 per cent (Women)
No: 56 per cent (Men) 55 per cent (Women)

However, the reasons for joining the gym differed slightly. Men claimed to want to improve their stamina. Women said they wanted to improve their shape.

All through this poll, the answers were amazingly similar. Questions were wide-ranging and covered topics such as relationships, sex, shopping, and friends. A surprising number of men use cosmetics and skincare preparations, and it becomes fairly obvious from the poll results why new houses are being built with more bathrooms and storage space for clothes. Another interesting fact is the subject of close friends.

The answers to this question were:
Number of close male friends: 5.5 (Men) 3.2 (Women)
Number of close female friends: 3.6 (Men) 5.7 (Women)
Total number of close friends: 8.9 (Men) 8.4 (Women)

So the average man has approximately nine close friends.

This circle of friends generally consists of both men and women, although it is weighted towards same-sex friendships. Men shed their friends as they get older. Women, by contrast, seem far better at retaining friendships as they age. It was also noted that singles of both genders tend to have significantly more friends than those with a partner.

'the answers were amazingly similar. questions were wide ranging and covered topics such as relationships, sex, shopping and friends'.

If we all have an average of eight or nine friends, then the ideas held in this course should be absolutely perfect for getting them together, having fun, sharing thoughts, emotions and faith and loving them into the kingdom. If your eight or nine friends are already Christians then clearly you all need to go out and meet more people. Though the authors of this book are both female, we have tried to offer a balance of ideas and observations. We have been encouraged by the answers in the poll as it shows that many of our ideas can be used by both men and women.

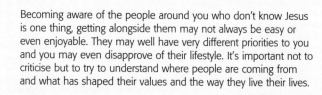

Becoming aware of the people around you who don't know Jesus is one thing, getting alongside them may not always be easy or even enjoyable. They may well have very different priorities to you and you may even disapprove of their lifestyle. It's important not to criticise but to try to understand where people are coming from and what has shaped their values and the way they live their lives.

If you read the account of the paragon of virtue in Proverbs 31 you will see a profile of the sort of lifestyle we might all aspire to, someone who juggles successful business transactions, keeps a firm hand on the domestic situation and has the respect of her children, and also maintains a happy, loving relationship with her husband. The struggle to manage those same three situations, work, family and relationships, is given as the primary cause of stress for modern women. Activate's Jill Lawson has re-written Proverbs 31 for the twenty-first century:

# does anyone understand women?

# ways of communicating with modern woman – who can find?

○ She is more complex than many microchips.

○ Her husband lost confidence in himself after his third redundancy and the man she lives with now is not her husband.

○ She brings to this relationship limited expectations, two children from an earlier marriage and one born out of wedlock.

○ Knitting needles she used to employ now act as props for her house-plants and her sewing machine has gone to the charity shop.

○ Many clothes she buys from mail-order catalogues.

○ She stays up late at night watching videos of soaps she has missed while at work during the day.

○ The family no longer eats together but puts instant snacks into the microwave.

○ She is not interested in buying a field but the publicity relating to a Time Share in Lanzarote tempts her.

○ Her arms are strong as twice a week she pumps iron at the leisure centre.

○ Her charitable giving is an emotional response to a visual appeal.

○ She needs tranquillisers to deal with the stress of juggling all the parts of her life.

○ Her teenagers rarely rise before noon at weekends and, in spite of all her sacrifices for them, her children call her...all sorts of names and their bedrooms resemble pigsties.

○ She laughs rarely, and fears of losing her current man are very real.

○ She considers suicide, and rape, mugging, cancer and loneliness are a constant fear.

○ The name of Jesus is often on her lips as a swear word.

○ This woman really needs to meet him.

○ But she may not, unless we introduce them.

So let's take a look at some different types of women and consider some of the underlying causes for their attitudes. During a session at the Activate conference 2003, Elaine Storkey gave some examples of four types of women she has come across and whose lives she has touched.

## the successful woman

Following a harrowing session in a radio studio, I went out into the anteroom and started to pray for the presenter, who'd been given a hard time. I suddenly became aware that there was someone else in the room. When I opened my eyes there she was. There had been a break for the news and she'd come out for a cup of coffee.

She asked what I was doing and I said I was praying for her. She said: 'Then don't let me stop you.' I continued praying as she sat quietly, and then I hugged her – something I've never done before although I've known her for fifteen years. She's not that sort of person. But she said 'We women need to stick together. I was so glad you were with me in there.' And I was able to share the gospel with her because she knew I had been listening. I had heard her and understood.

So when you're with the successful woman, look for the stories underneath, because often they will tell of the battles she's had to fight. If she's a particularly strident and objectionable person, it may be because she's had some tough battles and difficulties and somehow that stridency has become attached to her and she's been unable to peel it off. Then you can see if you can help her get back to her vulnerability. Create a safe place where she knows she won't get stabbed in the back or criticised. Go out of your way to get to know her and try to listen and relate.

## the struggling woman

This is a woman who is finding it hard to cope for all sorts of reasons. She might be OK most of the time, but she's just got too much on and is short of resources or needs to be relieved of some tasks.

She might be just too busy, not competent, she might be lacking in confidence because she's never made her own way, or she might be struggling with something in the past, something she hasn't been able to work through or get beyond and which needs some love and insight.

I know of one woman with a long history of abuse, who is asking, 'Where was God? I know he loves me now, I've experienced it now – but where was he in that abuse?' It's a question lots of women are asking, although they might not say it aloud. We need to hear the question, maybe ask it for them.

We need to be honest that we don't know all the answers, and some may need the help of an experienced counsellor. There will be someone you know who has suffered abuse in their background, statistically it's inevitable. For everyone who goes to see a counsellor there are two people who don't. So many people wear masks. Our task as Christians is not to judge, or worse still to advise them that they must forgive their abuser, but we can just be there to love them and be willing to listen.

## the woman facing new things

Women in this category often need help. Sometimes the situation they are facing is good or positive but it brings up feelings that are not happy. A poem called 'Poem to a First Grandson' by Phyllis Hill[10] speaks of the emotions experienced by a woman whose baby son died when he was a few hours old, when she first gazes upon her newborn grandson. Her words explain why there was a poignant, momentary pause before she responded in love to him.

Sometimes poetry helps to tap into the emotions, as the poet expresses things perhaps more easily than the person might. We may be able to use a poem to help someone vocalise or focus their feelings. People will sometimes happily share quite intimate details on buses and trains if they feel they are speaking to the right person. Sharing as a Christian means that people are brought into the orbit of God's love and God's blessing.

People facing new things or having old memories re-awakened will quite often need help. We may have to listen in different ways but don't be put off by their apparent anger or defiance. People sometimes need help in making decisions if they are at a crossroads in their life. They may be facing retirement or redundancy, moving jobs, getting married, or deciding about having children. Our role is reaching out, listening where they are and bringing God in.

Don't be afraid of affirming and praising people. Do be afraid of preaching, because they won't hear love, they'll just hear sermonising. They'll think we've got it all together when actually we're all needy people. We're sharing because we're Christians, not because we've got all the answers. We know that God loves us and Jesus died for us, so never be afraid of saying that or of praying for others.

## the angry woman

This final category of woman is the most difficult to be with. Bitter, bitchy people are draining and time with them needs to be rationed. Sometimes these women are so raw that we feel if the bitterness was taken away there would be nothing left. All we can do is listen to the reasons for the anger and try to address them and support the person.

I knew someone like this and because I listened to her reasons and addressed them the relationship changed for a while. However, I couldn't maintain a close link, and because her attitude was habitual she found it hard to move on. If you have a fairly constant relationship with an angry person you might be able to find ways to discover what it is that's 'eating them alive', but if you're very close, or if it's your mother for example, then you might not be the right person to help.

[10] Poem by Phyllis Hill published in: Lever and Lochhead, (eds.), ***West in her eye: Poems by women*** (Pyramid Press, 1995).

# what is

Obviously it's not just women who have to battle to be successful or who struggle with anger or change. Men struggle too, and because by nature they often find it more difficult to share on a deep level with friends, they can keep their problems and emotions locked away inside them. Possibly that's why men are so

*social trends might not have all the answers but can be a helpful barometer*

prone to heart attacks, high blood pressure and headaches. They are also equally vulnerable to stress and depression yet might not be as willing as women are to seek assistance, as the high rate of suicide among young men would seem to indicate.

Social trends might not have all the answers but can be a helpful barometer if we are seeking to find ways of helping others. So here are some facts and figures[11] to ponder:

[11] Social Trends – National statistics, Census 2001.

# stressing us out?

One in six people living in private households (not psychiatric patients) has been assessed as having symptoms of depression, anxiety or phobia. On average 19 per cent of women and 14 per cent of the men living in your area may well be suffering from these debilitating conditions and would be grateful for a helping hand.

In people aged 16-74 these were the reasons given for the illness or condition.

So, while there are many similarities and men are deeply affected by the death of loved ones too, there are other factors that make the genders different. As the statistics show, women are more likely to suffer from depression because of bereavement, separation, domestic violence or sexual abuse. Men worry more than women about redundancy, illness, bullying, violence at work or money. This could be because, in spite of modern trends, the majority of men still consider that it is their role to be the breadwinner. In this age of high spending and credit card debt, that puts a huge pressure on men. In a recent poll conducted by *The Guardian* newspaper it was clear that many women also felt that men should be the main breadwinners in the family. The poll also highlighted that, even in a

| EVENT | Male % | Female % |
| --- | --- | --- |
| Death of a close friend or relative | 68 | 73 |
| Death of a parent, child or partner | 51 | 55 |
| Sacked/redundant | 40 | 19 |
| Serious/life threatening illness | 30 | 22 |
| Breakdown of marriage/relationship | 25 | 29 |
| Bullying | 19 | 17 |
| Serious money problems | 14 | 8 |
| Violence at work | 6 | 2 |
| Running away from home | 5 | 5 |
| Violence at home | 4 | 10 |
| Homeless | 4 | 3 |
| Expelled from school | 2 | 1 |
| Sexual abuse | 2 | 5 |

# christians need to be open about their own feelings, giving others permission to do the same

relationship, women were willing to 'go dutch' and contribute to the expenses of an evening out, but very few indeed thought that women should pay for the date, even if they earned more than the men.

This often continues throughout relationships. Even if a relationship ends and the husband has moved out of the family home, whether that move was his choice or not, and there are children involved, the man has to go on providing. Some cases have clearly caused misery and hardship: having two homes means having two lots of bills, so break-ups can cause resentment and frustration.

The pressure group Fathers4Justice highlights the plight of men who find it difficult to get reasonable access to their children after the break-up of a marriage. Although a large percentage of women are now working full time, it is more usual for custody of children to be given to the mothers and some women can make life extremely difficult for dads, so they cannot have relaxed, fun times with their children or even see them. If fathers have to travel a long distance to see their children and have very little spare money, they can end up walking the streets with the children or trying to find activities that don't cost too much.

All these things conspire to make success and high earnings in the workplace a necessary goal. Redundancy is a nightmare that can easily become a reality. Perhaps that is why violence and bullying at work can be such major issues for men. They can feel less able to walk away from their jobs and become trapped in unpleasant or even abusive situations, possibly brought about by others in similar domestic positions jockeying for position and becoming overly competitive. Serious illness can also mean the loss of earnings and so the over-emphasis on the fear of illness reported in the statistics may well be linked to this whole work/life dynamic.

As Christians, we need to be aware of these spiralling situations and look for ways we can help. We can be vigilant in the workplace and not ignore situations in which someone is being treated unjustly. Bullying and harassment are serious but may only be dealt with if someone is willing to stand up as a witness.
Finally, Christians need to be open about their own feelings, giving others permission to do the same. Making it clear that we are willing to listen could make a huge difference to a man who might otherwise feel desperate and alone.

# what have you got in the house?

The question 'What have you got in the house?' reminds us of the story of Elisha and the widow in 2 Kings 4:1-7. The woman was destitute and desperate, and she turned to Elisha for help. He responded by asking her that very question.

> The wife of a man from the company of prophets cried out to Elisha, 'Your servant my husband is dead, and you know he revered the Lord. But now his creditor is coming to take my two boys as his slaves.'
>
> Elisha replied to her, 'How can I help you? Tell me, what do you have in your house?'
>
> 'Your servant has nothing here at all,' she said, 'except a little oil.'
>
> Elisha said, 'Go around and ask all your neighbours for empty jars. Don't ask for just a few. Then go inside and shut the door behind you and your sons. Pour oil into all the jars and as each is filled, put it to one side.'
>
> She left him and afterwards shut the door behind her and her sons. They brought the jars to her and she kept pouring.

When all the jars were full, she said to her son, 'Bring me another one.'

> But he replied, 'There is not a jar left.' Then the oil stopped flowing.
>
> She went and told the man of God and he said, 'Go, sell the oil and pay your debts. You and your sons can live on what is left.'

The widow's initial response was that she had nothing in the house at all, but then she told Elisha that she had a little oil. He encouraged her to take what little she had, and step out in faith. The woman obeyed without question or argument, even though it meant approaching the people around her to ask for jars.

This is a story with a happy ending. God honoured her obedience by making the oil flow until she had filled all the jars that she'd gathered from the neighbourhood. She was then able to resolve her difficulties, maintain her dignity and bring glory to God. Inspirational! But what can we learn by it? On a practical level, that God can use a little to make much more. Jesus demonstrated this beautifully, by catering for the masses with the contents of a small boy's lunch box. Hopefully we also learn that, however small and insignificant we consider our talents to be, God can use us in the building of the kingdom.

- What have you got in the house?
- Make a list of the fun things you enjoy.
- Do you only ever do these activities with other Christians?
- Could you include others?

We don't need to bring in experts to do evangelism, or sign up for exhaustive training courses that make outreach into a science. We just have to offer ourselves to God and ask him to give us opportunities to take his love into our community. He's made us who we are and planted us where we are. So don't worry about what gifts and skills you haven't got, just bring 'whatever you've got in the house' to God and be willing to approach the people around you. These can be neighbours, work colleagues, friends, those you meet at the gym, antenatal clinic or school gate or even, in times of crisis, the person in the next hospital bed.

Your circle of influence will be different at various points of life, so always be on the lookout for those who God might want you to include. Always be aware of the things others are interested in and be willing to join in their activities as well as inviting them to yours. Many people would agree that it is far more effective to join in with an existing group, and be 'salt and light' right there, than to start something new of our own. Let's take a look together around a house and see if this inspires you although most of these ideas can be used in any venue.

'The Word became flesh and blood and moved into the neighborhood'. This version of John 1:14 from *The Message*[12] reminds us beautifully of Jesus' role when he lived on earth. The problem now, for many of us, is that we often find it difficult to know where to start in building meaningful relationships with those around us. If you've lived in your road for fifteen years but had little contact with your neighbours, where do you begin? Let's look at a few stories of how some people got started.

## jenny and mike's story

The Macmillan Biggest Coffee Morning in the World (Tel: 0845 602 1246 for details) seemed like a perfect opportunity to get our neighbours together for the first time. Most of them were out at work all day so we held it on a Saturday. Although we'd lived in the house for twelve years we were only on nodding terms with most of them, and they didn't know each other either. Macmillan made it easy with ready-printed invitations, which had a space to write the people's names. This meant we had to knock on every door in our road to hand over the invitation personally. Everyone was friendly and told us their name, even if they weren't free to come to the event, which means we've been able to greet each other by name ever since.

An encouraging number came and we had loads of fun as the neighbours all got to know each other that day. As they were leaving someone said 'Let us know what you're doing next.' Since then, we've done the Samaritan's Purse Shoebox appeal, a pamper evening, a dinner party, a garden party and watched a film together. Finally we offered an *Alpha* course in our home, but only two neighbours came to that. So we need to continue the

relationship building as it seems to be most effective. Getting to know people has meant that they've shared problems and needs and they've been happy for us to pray with them. Two people have been healed of physical ailments and two other people have become Christians. Our neighbourhood now feels much more like a real community.

One of our neighbours, Mark, wrote the following letter to us, just a year after that first invitation to the Macmillan event. As you'll see from Mark's own account of his story, the pub is one of the places where he can have most influence, in his own inimitable style.

## mark's story

I started off being a rather ignorant witness because my friends would ask where I was on a Wednesday night, when I wasn't in the local with them. I must admit that in the beginning, I let pride stand in the way of honesty by saying that I had been seeing friends. Once I started to realise that Jesus was becoming an integral part of my life however, about three weeks into the course, I was honest and told them that I was attending a course which was aimed at people like me, who were interested in learning more about the Bible; almost like an idiot's guide to the Bible. I don't wish to sound rude when I use that comparison but having read several of the *Idiots' guide to...* books in the local library, I felt that this was a rather useful analogy when talking to my friends in the pub. I believe that *Alpha* is a very easy to understand introduction that enables the average guy in the street to study the videos, read certain parts of the Bible and think, yes, I understand this, this is what it's all about.

[12] Eugene H. Peterson, *The Message* (Colorado: Navpress, 2002).

Eventually, it was quite easy being honest to my friends. Most are pro-rugby players and are used to playing with colleagues from overseas who have a strong Christian faith, so it didn't seem strange for their mate to 'join the gang'. I found it harder talking to the older people I count among my friends. At first they were very sceptical which annoyed me, as they don't seem to have a problem with people in the pub who abuse their bodies on a regular basis. It seemed that they were almost jealous of me because I was participating in something that was against 'the norm'. I saw this as a very sad sign of the times. People take drugs or get drunk and no one seems to bother, yet just because you want to find out about Jesus, you get some so-called friends starting to raise their eyebrows!

I have since found that I don't have any trouble either being honest with people asking about my beliefs or striking up conversations with strangers about what *Alpha* has done for me as a person. Anyone who knows me will realise what a huge step this is, as I am a very quiet, shy lad. I believe that this inner strength comes from Jesus.

I have decided to have a tattoo of an image of Jesus, that has forever remained in my memory since I attended a Catholic school in the 1970s. Since having this tattoo, I have felt empowered in a funny kind of way. It has also provided me with a unique method of witnessing! When I have been in a gym, at the baths or on holiday, complete strangers ask to look closely at it. This gives them an opportunity to ask about my beliefs and allows me to explain my feelings and how my faith helps me in life. Indeed, on a recent trip to Spain, which is obviously a very Catholic country, I was stopped every fifty yards (or so it seemed) by locals interested in seeing my tattoo. They all crossed themselves on seeing and touching it, which I found to be a very moving experience. At home, it gives me the chance to discuss religion with people who might otherwise not feel the need to talk about it or who have no real inclination to even think about how religion could affect them on a day-to-day basis.

All this has come through joining the *Alpha* course. Although I was always religious, *Alpha* has given me the understanding required to interpret passages in the Bible that I can apply to my life. I am a better person because of this.

## tom's story

Tom was a student, studying for a degree and working in a pizza restaurant to supplement his student loan. One of his fellow waiters, Dave, was in his thirties and well travelled. His usual pattern was to stay in a place for six months or so and then move on, sometimes to another town, often to another country.

Tom and Dave often had interesting talks when business was slack and they shared a love of music. Dave was a Johnny Cash fan and he often pondered the meaning of the lyrics in his songs. One evening, while listening to *The Mercy Seat*, he was struck by the words and wanted to know more about what the mercy seat really was. The following evening as they served pizza together, Dave asked Tom what he knew.

Later that week Tom found himself at Dave's flat, Bible open, looking at all the Old Testament references to the mercy seat. Much discussion followed and although Dave has now moved on,

# 'the Word became flesh and blood and moved into the neighborhood' JOHN 1:14 FROM THE MESSAGE

the conversations he and Tom had, often based around Johnny Cash's songs, will be long remembered. Eternity may show that these were the beginning of something more.

Let's not make the mistake of having a secular/sacred divide in our lives. Let's remember that wherever we go, God has been there before us. He's working in the lives of those around us, in ways we may not understand. We simply need to be open to him and others and come alongside what he's doing.

*ask God to show you the possibilities as we go around this imaginary house*

# the front door

As we discover a host of different ideas, don't let the images of the different rooms distract you from the possibilities in your home. Some of us live in comparative luxury while others of us struggle to make ends meet. But whether you're a student trying to squash just one more person into your already heaving study-bedroom or have plenty of space, ask God to show you the possibilities as we go around the rooms of this imaginary house.

In Hebrews 13:2 we are commanded, 'Do not forget to entertain strangers, for by doing so, some people have entertained angels without knowing it.'

o How welcoming are you?

o Do you have a heart to reach out to others?

o Does your front door portray this?

If your door has no knocker, a bell that doesn't work and stickers announcing 'Beware of the Rottweiler', 'CCTV – You are being watched', 'No Callers without prior appointment' or 'Keep Out!' then your neighbours might think twice before calling to see you for a friendly chat. Some of the grander new developments that are being built offer high security, maid and shopping facilities. The people inside need never venture into the outside world. The level of security and service on offer surely means there is a risk of making the residents feel imprisoned. We need to keep a sense of proportion about safety issues. And, even if we can't literally leave our doors open, we can have an 'open door' mentality and be willing to open our homes and hearts to people.

It's not always going to be easy and, inevitably, you'll enjoy the company of some people more than others. There is much truth in the Portuguese proverb: 'A guest always brings pleasure: if not the arrival, the departure'. We've probably all experienced the dilemma of the party that seems endless.

# the hall

We've already seen that the staircase (steps) can be used as a useful visual aid, to signify the journey of faith. The ideas in this book are pitching on the bottom five steps and are about getting alongside and building relationships with people who have little or no knowledge of God. When Christians get to know people and build relationships with them, they effectively take people from steps 1 and 2 onto step 3 – contact with Christians. The person has moved a step up the staircase before you begin to share anything.

Then we pray that, through positive contact with Christians, those within our circle of influence will begin to be interested in Jesus (step 4) and eventually decide to investigate Jesus (step 5). It is at this stage that we pray they will be keen to investigate the Christian faith further.

As C.S. Lewis observed in his classic work, *Mere Christianity*, people are not 100 per cent Christian or 100 per cent non-Christian. Some are moving from being Christians, others are moving towards Christ. Lewis was pointing out something he believed to be plainly obvious, not only from his experience of life, but also from his reading of the words of Jesus – things just aren't that clear. Shorthand terms like Christian and non-Christian may at first appear useful but you soon realise that they can cause us to miss the point. As far as Jesus was concerned, it is evident that it wasn't how close someone was to him at any given stage in their life that mattered, as much as the direction in which they were travelling. Judas, for example, shared some of Jesus' most intimate moments; he was one of the inner community of twelve, right up until the Last Supper. For anyone looking in from the outside, his relationship with Jesus would have appeared close, but begin to scratch away the surface and you would have soon discovered that he was heading away from Jesus rather than being drawn closer – he was travelling in the wrong direction. In the end, only God knows where anyone really stands with him.

## the telephone table

It's good to talk – and your telephone can be a means of bringing God's love into other people's lives. Those who are housebound or have long-term illnesses can often feel forgotten and a cheery phone call can be a great tonic. Someone who might be embarrassed by prayer face-to-face will often be really blessed if you pray for them over the phone. Even if you can't get out much yourself you'll be able to do this. So do think about ringing someone who is lonely and bring a bit of God's love into their day.

## your phone book

Everyone knows a circle of people who know a circle of people, who know a circle of people. Through one very positive contact you could reach as many as 250 by word-of-mouth recommendations. We might be willing to do this if we got really good service or a superb bargain, but what about the good news of the gospel? How many of our friends, neighbours and colleagues do we want to see come to a living faith in Jesus? Eternal life is a free gift to all but we tend to feel it costs us our reputation to tell others.

You will have a circle of influence that is uniquely yours, whether that's the people in your office, the parents at the school gate or the houses directly around yours. It's a clear case of it's not what you know, but who you know. That's why we want to suggest lots of easy ways to meet people and to enjoy each others' company while pursuing shared interests. It almost doesn't matter what you do as long as you get together and get to know others.

As you start to build relationships with others they will begin to be real with you. Hopefully, they will see something different or special about you that will prompt them to ask questions and give you the opportunity to share something of your life with them. Simply be ready to answer their questions. As 1 Peter 3:15 says, 'Always be prepared to give an answer to everyone who asks you to give the reason for the hope that you have.'

## hats, coats, gloves, scarves & boots

You won't always want to stay in with friends. The hall is where you hang everything you need to step out into the great outdoors. Walking has been proven to be the best exercise ever. It trims your hips and thighs, strengthens your lungs and heart, and sparkles up dull hair, skin and eyes. If you're a fair-weather walker, remember that exercising in cold air burns off more calories than it does in summertime. It is also a great opportunity to talk. Many of Jesus' discussions took place on the move. People are often much more relaxed about asking questions and discussing things when you are walking side by side, instead of sitting face to face.

So why not rally some ramblers, or lead a dog walk? It's much safer walking together than alone and can be great fun. Maybe the group could take turns at finding new routes and organising trips further afield.

Stand at the crossroads and look; ask for the ancient paths, ask where the good way is, and walk in it, and you will find rest for your souls. (Jer. 6:16)

# the lounge

Take a look around your lounge. Is the seating grouped around the television, making it the focal point of the room? Technology is a wonderful thing and most of us in the UK have access to information and entertainment through our televisions, with some houses having several sets. Rather than watch the TV in isolation, you might consider using your viewing as an outreach opportunity...

## television

In a recent lifestyle survey 99 per cent of both men and women said that their favourite relaxation was watching TV. Some programmes require very little of us other than to sit passively and watch – though soaps are a great source of discussion. If you see something worth recording you can catch the omnibus edition later.

Sports programmes are good communal watching, so why not invest in a large screen television and guarantee that your house will be a favoured venue for sports events such as football and Wimbledon. You could easily extend this to include quiz shows and debates.

As Christians we often miss vital opportunities to have a voice. The BBC launched a poll inviting viewers and listeners to vote for their favourite Briton, who would then have an hour-long programme dedicated to their life and work by a sympathetic presenter. It was obvious from the results that very few Christians had bothered to take part, which led Elaine Storkey to comment on this issue in *The Christian Herald*.

The Great Britons series was such a good idea! It provided an opportunity for every group with a cause, whether political, philosophical or simply cultic, to nominate their founder. It must have taken some effort on behalf of the Welsh Nationalists to nudge Owen Glendower into one place ahead of the Queen! The series came at a time when we needed to be reminded of our past, and those who have made a significant contribution to our history and culture, but significant names are missing from the last ten. Key people who made a very obvious Christian impact came lower down. William Tyndale, Lord Shaftesbury, John Wesley, William Wilberforce all featured briefly, but there's no doubt we have missed an opportunity. With more effort from Christians, the BBC could have been commissioning a first class documentary of someone whose life had Jesus Christ at its very centre.

Had Tyndale got a better backing it would have been impossible to tell his story without acknowledging the pivotal commitment of his life, his belief in God and the truth of God's word. It would have been unthinkable to evaluate his legacy without recognizing that for hundreds of years this affected the very structure and belief of our nation. Viewers could have been given a new perspective of the Christian faith if just ten per cent of church attenders had voted for those who have played a key Christian part in our British heritage.

So why didn't we vote? Why did we leave the take up to the general population who didn't mind getting stuck in? It could be that we thought we had better things to do with our time, or that most of us are not particularly interested in who people think are important – we have our own ideas and that's good enough for us. It could be that our energies are too taken up with church issues and wrangles. Or it could be that we think we are 'above' the tedious media circus: the soap operas, phone-ins and personality cults. We don't see ourselves as part of this ritual and frankly we don't want to be part of the popular culture.

If this is the case then we have paid a high price. We have failed to take hold of something offered to us on a plate. At the same time that Christian broadcasting companies struggle for funds and audiences, this series penetrated the mainstream and spoke to millions. At the same time that we moan there is nothing good on television, this series gave us the opportunity to use our sheer numbers to vote for something else. At the same time we despair that the popular culture never presents Christian truth with any kind of sympathy, we turned down the opportunity to make this a real possibility. In short, we blew it. We did not spot the chance.

This means that, sadly, the story of Great Britons was only partly told. Even with a series as good as this, the real truth of where we have come from will not yet be presented on our screens. The responsibility remains with us. Having missed this one, let's keep our eyes more open to our culture and be more vigilant next time.

## useful phone numbers - try to use them more to congratulate than to complain.

### Ofcom
Tel: 0845 456 3000 or 0207 981 3040; fax 0845 456 3333. Website www.ofcom.org.uk or email contact@ofcom.org.uk or write to: Ofcom Contact Centre, Riverside House, 2a Southwark Bridge Road, London, SE1 9HA. Ofcom is the independent regulator and competition authority for the UK communications industries, with responsibilities across television, radio, telecommunications and wireless communications services.

### BBC
Tel: 0870 010 0222 – email info@bbc.co.uk for comments and general information.

### ITV Network Ltd
Tel: 020 7843 8000 email info@itv.co.uk for comments about independent television, or contact your local ITV Company.

### British Board of Film Classification
Tel: 0207 353 1248

### The Media Awareness Project (MAP)
Tel: 0207 222 5533 email action@themothersunion.org

### Advertising Standards Authority
Tel: 0207 580 5555

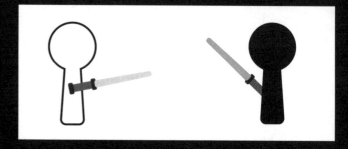

## film club

Films are a great way of sparking thoughts and discussion. So why not join a group in your area or start your own film group? You could begin by inviting everyone to bring a short film clip (maximum five minutes) which they feel outlines their worldview. They can give a short introduction to explain what they are going to show, which must not be longer than their clip. After this you can agree on the next film – ask everyone to watch it in advance and show clips to discuss; or you can continue to bring clips from films or soap operas and share thoughts. Log on to the Damaris website, www.damaris.org, for details of a range of contemporary films and discussion questions.

If you feel your guests are ready for a slightly more up-front message, then why not lend them a Christian film? *Tales from the Madhouse* contains atmospheric and arresting monologues by characters who had contact with Jesus: People like the thief on the cross, the centurion, the wife of Pontius Pilate and Judas, the betrayer. It is available for £13.99 plus £2.50 postage and packing from the Bible Society, c/o Marston Christian Books, PO Box 269, Abingdon, Oxon OX14 4YN or ring 0500 555 802.

Mel Gibson's *The Passion* was a major box office success which generated lots of discussion. It may be more appropriate to lend this video out and then discuss it informally at a later date.

## or you could simply switch off

The advantages of being more informed and entertained can be outweighed by the lack of communication that can result when a family watches television constantly. It can easily become a conversation killer. So why not switch off your set and play a board game occasionally? If you invite others to join in you might be pleasantly surprised at the response. Board games such as Scrabble are growing in popularity again and they have been mentioned by superstars as being great boredom-busters when they are waiting about during rehearsals.

Unplugging the television gives opportunity to chat and make a cup of coffee a social event, so why not try some of the following ideas in your lounge and see what the take-up is in your neighbourhood?

## discussion groups

Steve and Jane hold a Talkback group in their home every fortnight. Everyone brings something to the group that has made them feel 'Mad, Sad, Bad or Glad' since they last met. This might be a newspaper cutting, a poem or extract from a book, a piece of music or film clip, a photo, a personal situation or even a box of treasured memories.

Talkback groups give the opportunity for lively discussion, followed by drinks and refreshments, and there's rarely enough time to cover everything that the participants want to say. The issues of life and death are always on the agenda and the Christians in the group often have an opportunity to share something of their faith or occasionally to pray for others.

## charity/coffee events

These are excellent starters if you want to begin inviting people into your home. You probably need an excuse or an occasion to start the ball rolling. The Macmillan Biggest Coffee Morning in the World is held at the end of September every year. Posters, invitations, recipes, a quiz and money off coupons for coffee and biscuits are provided. A Friday morning is specified for the event but you can hold it at any convenient time for yourself and intended guests. Other charities and organisations arrange similar events, which can be held at different times in the year.

## achkiy parties

The word 'Achkiy' is a native Peruvian word meaning 'anything that shines', reflecting how the Achkiy project (started in 1996 by Julia Castle, Fiona's daughter) is bringing light and hope to the lives of many. Julia has encouraged and taught women from a shanty town near Lima, Peru to make jewellery using gemstones and top quality silver. They also use recycled paper to make attractive hand-made cards, notebooks and bookmarks, which they sell at about half the price of similar products in British commercial card shops.

Anyone can consider having an Achkiy party in their home as a way of getting to know their neighbours and sending much needed funds to this project. It costs nothing to have an Achkiy party. Invitations, a selection of products on a sale or return basis and a twelve-minute video demonstrating the work are supplied, so you don't even have to try to explain it to your friends. The response has been overwhelmingly positive; lots of people from schoolchildren to grannies have held parties in homes, workplaces and school fairs, which has made a huge impact in Peru, but also is helping to break the ice in neighbourhoods all around the country. Ring the Activate office (Tel: 01384 370775 or email info@activatecv.org.uk) for more information and details of how you can hold a party in your area.

## well women workshops

Well Women Workshops are a series of sessions designed to encourage women coming out of depression, bereavement, abusive situations, mental illness or those just needing a new challenge. The aim of the workshops is for women to grow in self-awareness, confidence and self-esteem and to begin to see life from other perspectives. Women are encouraged to be more 'others centred', to focus on giving and hospitality, and to make lasting friendships with others who may be like-minded.

The workshops are a course of eight sessions held in a home setting, where a group of six to ten women meet together to discuss physical, emotional and spiritual well-being, as well as issues around home versus employment and creativity and social awareness. Referrals come informally by personal recommendation, or by just chatting with people, and formally from health centres, social services and other voluntary organisations that provide services for women. Rarely a day goes by without the organisers receiving a phone call from one agency or other inquiring about what Well Women Workshops do.

Three Christian women run the workshops but they are keen not to 'push' Christianity on those who attend the group but prefer to speak of their experience of God through their own personal testimonies.

Many women feel isolated within their homes. They may be new mothers, their children may have just started full-time school, they may have retired early because of ill health or they may have recently retired because of their age. Feelings of isolation can lead to depression and a sense that their situation is beyond repair. There's a saying that 'a problem shared is a problem halved' and Well Women Workshops find that women enjoy going into a home environment to chat, drink coffee and eat cake! The three trainers speak about their own personal challenges with great honesty and this helps the women to be honest about their own struggles and to see that there are other people in similar or even worse situations. They speak about deep issues and they cry but they also have lots of fun. Finding a balance is essential for everyone's sanity!

If you are interested in running a series of Well Women Workshops in your local area, contact Jill via the Activate office: Tel: 01384 370775.

## well women workshop stories

For the first time in five years I feel I am beginning to live and not just exist. To feel the fear and do it anyway, to take risks.

In the past twelve years I have been through an emotional war. I felt a failure, worthless, a victim and my self-esteem was about as high as a slug's belly on a paving stone. I attended these Workshops which have been so helpful – they have challenged my perception of others and myself and I realise there are others in the same position suffering as much pain and looking for friends and support. I am building friendships which are healthy and wholesome, in spite of being demoralised by fear, and beginning to fill the dark corners of my life with some light and hope. The Workshops have changed my life. They are a

safe, caring and supportive environment where I have opened up and shared, without feeling judged. They have opened my 'eyes' and my 'heart'. I am in the process of positive change and personal growth. They have helped me gain confidence, self-esteem, and focus. It's a very special place to be, where everybody respects each other. All the trainers have been immensely supportive, caring, honest, encouraging, empathetic, non-judgemental and inspiring. They have all given me the confidence to begin those crucial steps forward, to take risks, to get out there and live! They all made me feel safe, worthy and really special.

I've never been to a group meeting before. I was very shy but received a warm welcome. Everyone in the group was very kind and made it easy for me to fit in. I felt relaxed; I was looking forward to the next week. We have lunch together and chat. I am going to miss the group but all good things must come to an end and I will keep in touch.

Another woman was recently bereaved, having cared for her mother for a year. She is a young Moslem mum whom Jill, one of the organisers, met in the school playground. She had to force herself out of her house in order to take her son to school. Jill noticed that she looked rather lost and befriended her, and gently persuaded her that the Workshops might be just what she needed. She reluctantly agreed and gleaned so much from the group. By the end of the course she was perfectly comfortable leading exercises from the flip chart. She looked good. She had her hair done. She went on to do voluntary work in the school, is now doing a counselling course, and is a different woman who is now looking out for people herself in order to befriend them.

# the kitchen

However high or low you might rank in celebrity cook status, there is no doubt that the kitchen is the heart of the home, and there is something about the casual intimacy of this inner sanctum that invites shared confidences. Tea and sympathy are a heady mix over the warm security of the kitchen table. Transport the action into the relative formality of the lounge and the atmosphere is completely different.

## cookery

So why not make a date for a regular one-to-one in your kitchen with a friend? If you feel guilty just sitting or haven't got the time you could plan to do your ironing or cook together as you chat and use the time productively. Some Christians have given time and cookery skills to lead a small class – either in their own homes or in the local community centre at a family support group. They give advice on nutrition or cooking on a budget and demonstrate easy recipes. It's good fun, a way of sharing your gifts and everyone gets to take something home for tea.

## cottage café

Did you know that a recipe for spicy ginger and pumpkin soup could help slave girls in Ghana achieve freedom and a new life? Or that a portion of celery and leek broth might bring help to the street children of Calcutta? For the past twenty years, Christine Morey has run her own school for machine knitting but it's a dying art and many machines lie idle and unwanted around the country. Christine has collected hundreds of machines, cleaned and

repaired them and sent them to centres as far apart as Ghana and Romania. She follows later to teach women how to use the machines to support their families. Christine has produced a recipe book, *The Cottage Café Super Soups*, and the proceeds from the sale of the book help the project continue.

The recipe for Tuscan Bean Soup shows a smiling girl knitting in a Romanian orphanage, where over forty machines have been placed and forty girls trained to use them. They knit items for the other 480 girls, including their underwear. Cauliflower, Bacon and Stilton soup is linked to young Ukrainians where the women barter the items they have knitted in the street markets where they can exchange a jumper for a rabbit or a dozen eggs. Twenty machines have gone to Calcutta, where women at a day centre in the city knit for pavement children who visit the centre. Orders are taken for knitwear and the women are making a small income from their craft.

In Ghana, young girls from the Troski tribe are sold into slavery and bonded to the priests to become their domestic and sexual slaves. Deeply traumatised, these girls are rejected by their families and often end up as prostitutes facing almost certain death from Aids. Centres have been established to train these women in skills to earn a living and the knitting machines have produced prized, unusual items which can readily be sold. Contact Christine Morey (Tel: 01803 555759) for a copy of *The Cottage Café Super Soup Book* and think of creative ways of using these recipes in your community.

## bread making

One Methodist minister in Liverpool has set up bread-making sessions as an alternative way of doing church. When the bread is in the oven everyone gathers to consider a Bible passage. Participants are invited to offer prayers for themselves or others and to light one of a collection of candles in a large dish on the table. Afterwards, some of the bread is eaten at a community meal and local churches distribute the rest.

Why not try gathering a group to make bread? Kneading the dough is a great way to get rid of anger and frustration and the space created whilst waiting for the dough to rise and the bread to bake can become a discussion group session. Afterwards, you can share the bread with cheese, salad and some home-made soup. Consider linking this with *The Cottage Café Super Soup* Book.

## chocolate parties

Judy organised a chocolate party at a local hotel, but this idea works just as well in a home.

She writes, 'The bar was open as people arrived for a drink which was included in the ticket price and we began with a few facts about chocolate, comparative calories, why it is good for you and gave "permission" for everyone to be off diet for the evening! We showed two short video clips (about three minutes long) from the film *Chocolat* and there was an opportunity to discuss the issues it raised. This was followed by a video demonstration by Delia Smith of the truffle torte from her *Winter Collection*. We didn't have the facilities for an actual demonstration but the video worked well. We had a number of tables set up around the outside of the room with tried and tested recipes for tasting – everything in small portions, with plastic plates and teaspoons - lots of things to try, including the truffle torte.

We managed to gather ten chocolate fondue sets with tea lights underneath to keep the chocolate melted. With each fondue was a platter of fresh fruit pieces and the visual effect was quite stunning. Information was available about Fair Trade chocolate and other goods and there was the opportunity to take part in some fun activities such as guessing the number of Smarties in a jar and chocolate quizzes. We had stations for tea, coffee and hot chocolate and while guests were enjoying their drinks, they sat down and marked the quizzes – the answers were up on a screen to save time. Prizes were given out and the whole evening was a great success.'

A small group using a home might make chocolates or Easter eggs using moulds, which can be purchased at a reasonable cost. Contact the Home Chocolate Factory on 0208 939 9000 (www.homechocolatefactory.co.uk) for details.

## fair trade

Contact Traidcraft on 01869 355100 (www.oxfam.org.uk) for a selection of fairly traded chocolate.

Fair Trade events are always popular. Logging on to a site such as www.fairtrade.org.uk (Tel: 0207 405 5942) will give up-to-the-minute information on events nationwide and ideas on how to get involved. Fair Trade fortnight is usually held at the beginning of March each year.

## fruto del espirito

Fruto del Espirito was set up to open up new overseas markets for exotic fruit and fruit products, increasing production, generating employment and contributing to sustainable development in Colombia. A Fruto del Espirito event combines supporting a Fair Trade project in Colombia with a fun evening tasting and drinking a variety of fruit purees. It includes a demonstration of how the fruits can be used to make exciting desserts and drinks which provide a good talking point. It also raises awareness of the plight of the two million people in Colombia who have lost homes, farms, livelihoods and family as a result of the extreme violence in the country, which is often financed by the drug trade. Investment in the fruit industry contributes to peace, offering a future and a hope to small farmers and displaced people.

A group in Thame organised a Fruto del Espirito event on a cold January evening. The hot-spiced fruit drinks ('calientes') were very welcome, and the guests wandered about, chatting and looking at the posters and literature on display. Rutie, who set up the project, gave an excellent and inspiring talk about the fruits of Colombia and her aspirations for the business. Everyone who came agreed that it had been a great way to entertain friends – a bit like a fun cocktail party. What is more, they were inspired to spend generously, because they really liked the fruit puree products.

A DVD and recipes are available, making it possible for individuals or a small group to organise a tasting event in a home.

Contact Rutie Stranack on 01277 363215 or email info@fruto.co.uk for more information about holding a Fruto del Espirito event in your area.

## healthy eating

We're all now very conscious of what we eat and 'Healthy Eating' is a great platform for a variety of events, from discussing one of the many new food related books to swapping ideas for children's lunch boxes.

# the dining room

'Strange to see how a good dinner and feasting reconciles everyone.' *The Diary of Samuel Pepys*[13].

In the last UK national census, people were asked to list their favourite leisure activities.[14] Watching television came out on top across the board (99 per cent) but a close second, 97 per cent for women and 95 per cent for men, was having a meal with friends. Food is a common denominator; we all have to eat. This can be a perfunctory exercise, absent-mindedly eating a sandwich while opening the post or watching TV or it can be made into a pleasurable social occasion by sitting around with friends. You don't have to go overboard with the catering, unless you really enjoy cooking. Just serve simple food so that you can relax and enjoy the evening. You can even share the catering and let others bring the pudding. People tend to come for the company, not the food. If cooking isn't your thing, buy a take-away or ready meal and assemble it yourself. You can use traditional events as excuses for a grand meal, such as Thanksgiving and Christmas, and choose your menu accordingly.

Let others share in the preparation or the washing up if they volunteer – you can have great conversations while peeling carrots or wiping dishes. The aim is to get to know people, not to exhaust yourself trying to be a faultless hostess, which can intimidate others. You could invite neighbours from other cultures to bring samples of their traditional dishes.

[13] *The Times Book of Quotations* (London: HarperCollins, 2000). [14] National Statistics, Census 2001.

## thanksgiving dinner

Guy was leading a project with three others some years ago. They were travelling the country and working long hours at the office to meet deadlines, so his wife, Caroline, suggested he got the team together with their partners for dinner to give everyone a chance to get to know each other socially.

They all got along really well and after that first evening, another person offered to cook a meal a couple of months later. They were never legalistic about it, as they agreed that social ping-pong could be a pain if you don't feel like joining in, but everyone felt that it was a good idea to meet regularly. Even though the project finished years ago, they have continued to meet as friends. The other three couples were not Christians and one husband was fairly 'anti' at first, though he was never unfriendly, but gradually he began to thaw and chat easily with Guy and Caroline about their faith. His wife became a Christian recently and they all went to the service when she was confirmed in their local Anglican church. They've now all been to church together occasionally on special occasions.

This year Guy and Caroline decided to invite the rest of the group for a meal in November and suggested a dinner at Thanksgiving. Everyone was asked to come with something in mind that they were thankful for in their lives and they all seemed very happy with this. The team just chatted as usual over the meal, and the things that they were grateful for came out very naturally. The topics included health, relationships, children and leisure so there was no strain or embarrassment involved. At the end of the meal Caroline just said she wanted to say a brief prayer and thanked God for their lives and all the things they appreciated and enjoyed.

There wasn't any blinding flash of lightning for anyone but it was a good opportunity for people to express gratitude and for them to see Caroline pass those thoughts to God in a relaxed chatty way, rather than the formal churchy manner they possibly expected.

This kind of event is seed sowing. The group accepts Guy and Caroline because they are fond of them as friends, and through that association, God comes into focus occasionally and naturally. On one occasion, Caroline rang one of the wives because she was on her mind. It was a timely call because she was very low about something and her husband later commented that he found it amazing that Caroline had been prompted to ring her just at that moment. God is in with a good chance with this gang!

## socialising with work colleagues

Dave met Andy through a colleague at work and over the course of a few weeks they had some conversations about the Christian faith. One day Andy told Dave he'd been talking to some of his other friends about their conversations and invited Dave to a supper party he was planning, so he could tell these friends what he believed.

Dave discovered that the other guests included two neo-pagans, into tarot cards and conspiracy theories, an ex-Hindu, two arty types, and a seriously ill ex-serviceman partnered by a business consultant thirty years his junior. One was a bell-ringing author who didn't like people disagreeing with him, and another, in the legal profession, was an atheist and heavily into politics. Dave was given five minutes to explain what Christianity is about and then it was over to the other guests for questions and chat.

The conversation which followed covered other religions, suffering, how can you know God exists, surely as long as you're spiritual that's all that matters? The neo-pagans tried to evangelise Dave with their brand of New Age spirituality and the ex-Hindu asked questions after question. Many issues were gently probed by razor sharp minds that managed to stay lucid after more alcohol than should have been possible.

These are people in our society. Most have virtually no contact with Christian things but are into spirituality in a variety of ways. This event reminds us just how far removed the majority of people today are from Christian thinking and Christian people.

Consider:
- How open are people to talking about spiritual things if they're approached in the right way?

- What impact do you think you would have had, if you had been in Dave's position?

- How vital is it to engage with people where they are comfortable and not where we're comfortable?

## charity dinners

Charitable events are hugely popular. Marie Curie Cancer Care suggest holding dinner parties and charging £5.00 per head, on the basis that three guests will raise funds for one hour of nursing care (£15.00) for a cancer patient. Look out for other suggestions on television and in the press that could be adapted to your social circle. Consider throwing simple fun suppers such as pizza or pancake parties to launch the start of Lent and ask everyone to bring fillings and topping ingredients.

## curry suppers

Curry suppers are an easy way of informal entertaining. Cook the meal together or phone for a take-away to be delivered to your door.

## murder mystery evenings

How about hosting a murder mystery dinner? These are great fun and there are lots of these on the market at the moment for about £15-£20. Once you've done a few you'll be confident enough to write your own. You can also download games, catering for groups as small as six and as large as 200, from www.murdermysterygames.co.uk.

The game boxes usually contain invitations, recipe ideas and all the items you need to run the evening, including a taped message from the Inspector and a running programme of hints and tips for each role. There are lots of different ways to have fun in a murder mystery evening and you'd be amazed at the different side of people that comes out when they are in costume and playing a role. It's a great way to break the ice with neighbours and friends.

If you want a slightly larger organised event, these are often put on by hotels around the country: some even run them as murder weekends. At these events each table constitutes a team who act as detectives and observe vital clues. The action is played out throughout the evening between courses. At the end of the evening the cast come into the room and are summoned to each table in turn to be interrogated. The cast then judge the tables for who worked well as a team and how pertinent their questions were.

You might try organising an event like this yourself and bringing in a team of actors to entertain you with a murder played out in your midst. The best arrangement is a circle of tables of up to ten people at each, with a space in the middle for the drama. This is a unique combination of theatre, improvisation and audience involvement for groups of up to 120. Obviously there is a fee involved but people will usually be happy to pay for a ticket to such a fun evening – especially if there is good food thrown in.

It's guaranteed to provide a talking point afterwards. Contact The Murder Squad on 01772 257174 www.themurdersquad.co.uk.

## afternoon tea

Afternoon tea is making a comeback, so dig out your pretty china and scone recipes. It's an inexpensive way of entertaining and everyone gets home before dark. Why not sample some of the herbal teas and posh teas on sale in the shops? Simple cakes can be bought from the supermarket and icing, fruit or chocolate added. It might be an ideal time for your craft or reading group to meet on a Saturday or Sunday or during the week if the members are not out at work.

Jesus recognised the value of eating with friends and that people are more relaxed and more receptive to new ideas when they are eating, so food played a major part in his ministry. The details of our Holy Communion rituals were set out after a Passover meal. Peter was commissioned to 'feed my sheep' during a fish barbecue on the beach. And Jesus chose to pitch some of his most potent teaching during the Feast of Tabernacles when the crowds would be at maximum capacity. When he fed the 5,000, they turned up in droves the next day to hear him. People love to be fed – and

attendance at events is always higher when there is food included. So why not open up your dining room, get some assistance from Delia, and see what God can do with your guests through the conversations you have.

*'better a meal of vegetables where there is love than a fattened calf with hatred'* (Prov. 15:17).

# the library

'What is the use of a book, thought Alice, without pictures or conversation?' *Alice's Adventures in Wonderland* – Lewis Carroll[15]

Few homes are grand enough to have a library, but most of us have a collection of books and a quiet place in our homes to curl up and read. Freedom to read can be limited by the demands of a busy career, caring for children or the elderly. Many of us feel guilty while reading a chapter of a novel during daylight hours when there is a stashed in-tray to be dealt with or chores still to be done. But if it really was for freedom that Christ has set us free, then we should allow ourselves a little relaxation.

## reading groups

The Reading group was possibly inspired by the Holy Spirit as a wonderful forum for sharing our faith without the aid of a soapbox. Secular books are full of issues of morality, choices, life and death and loneliness and you'll have some brilliant opportunities to share some of your views. Reading, according to the 2004 General Household Survey for the Office of National Statistics survey, is the latest craze to sweep Britain, yet it's been around for thousands of years. Reading is now the fourth most popular leisure activity in this country and frequent discussions of the latest novels on daytime TV shows has led people around the country to get together and discuss their favourites.

When the BBC launched *The Big Read* it was an opportunity for the public to vote for their favourite book, culminating in a top ten debate, with star names championing the literary rivals. The public's top one hundred books were revealed, launching several months of concentrated reading, during which people were encouraged to swap and talk about their favourite reads. The top ten books were featured, with ten programmes each profiling one book in depth. The BBC 2 Controller, Jane Root, hoped the idea would catch the public imagination and inspire people to set up book clubs up and down the country. 'We are trying to turn a private experience into something people do together. I have this fantasy that you get on the tube in the morning and everyone is reading the same book.'

This vision has recently been taken up in Liverpool, where there was a campaign to get everyone reading the book *Holes*.[16] The local libraries stocked up on it and bookshops were offering big reductions. The hope was that people would buy a copy and then leave it on a bus or park bench and someone who couldn't afford to buy one could then pick it up – making the project accessible to everyone. There was a similar initiative in Manchester and people were invited to donate their favourite books. The idea was to write your name and the date inside the cover and others would do the same, so that you could see how many people had read the book. Drop off points were designated all over the city. Community ideas

---

[15] *The Times Book of Quotations* (London: HarperCollins, 2000). [16] Louis Sachar, *Holes* (Collins Educational, 2001).

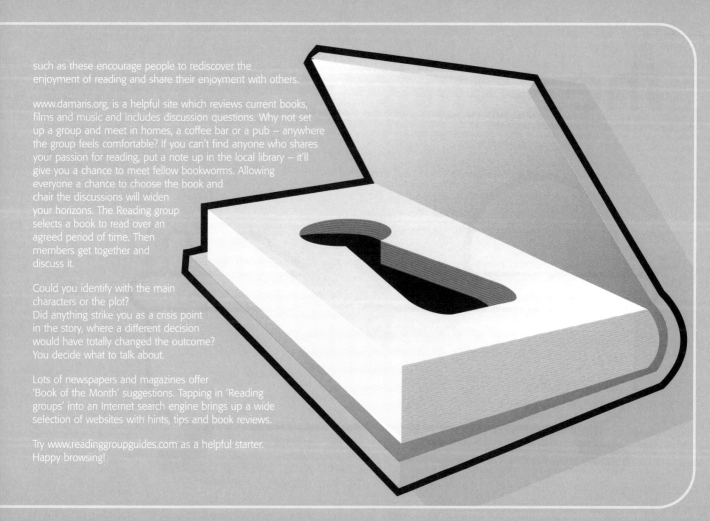

such as these encourage people to rediscover the enjoyment of reading and share their enjoyment with others.

www.damaris.org, is a helpful site which reviews current books, films and music and includes discussion questions. Why not set up a group and meet in homes, a coffee bar or a pub – anywhere the group feels comfortable? If you can't find anyone who shares your passion for reading, put a note up in the local library – it'll give you a chance to meet fellow bookworms. Allowing everyone a chance to choose the book and chair the discussions will widen your horizons. The Reading group selects a book to read over an agreed period of time. Then members get together and discuss it.

Could you identify with the main characters or the plot?
Did anything strike you as a crisis point in the story, where a different decision would have totally changed the outcome?
You decide what to talk about.

Lots of newspapers and magazines offer 'Book of the Month' suggestions. Tapping in 'Reading groups' into an Internet search engine brings up a wide selection of websites with hints, tips and book reviews.

Try www.readinggroupguides.com as a helpful starter.
Happy browsing!

# the bathroom

In the *Female Lifestyle Survey 2004*[17] over eight out of ten women said they wished they could change their lives. According to statistics, their mundane and tiring lives are driving some women to hit the bottle and raid the fridge in an attempt to de-stress. Each generation seems to identify its own crippling health and social problems and as we look at the lives of twenty-first century women it seems that stress is one of the top ranking problems of our time. So any de-stressing ideas are sure to prove popular, not only with us but also with those we work with and live near. A one-off event or a series covering stress-related issues is something that's sure to be welcomed in any area as long as it's timed to fit in with people's busy schedules.

One group organised a couple of successful Saturday morning workshops under the title 'Understanding Yourself' and covered themes such as 'How to cope with stress', 'How to build your self esteem', 'How to communicate effectively' and 'How to break free from being a people pleaser'. Sessions such as these would be relevant to both men and women. Spa Parties, pampering events and makeovers can all give the opportunity for meaningful conversations in a relaxed atmosphere, where women will often talk openly about some of the issues they're struggling with. These can be home-grown events, even using store cupboard ingredients or you can bring in the experts using party plan, such as a Virgin Vie consultant (Tel: 0845 300 8022) or Body Shop at Home (0845 05 0607).

Most stress-busting articles include the suggestion of 'setting aside some quiet time' to balance the noise and confusion which invades much of our time, so biblical meditation, prayer or reading a few verses from a modern version of the Bible might be

acceptable as part of a stress-busting event. The bathroom is a great place to unwind, especially if you have a good selection of beauty products to pour into a deep bath, and there are so many wonderful products to choose from, even in the budget ranges. Beauty is big business and this area accounts for a high level of spending by some women and increasing numbers of men.

Nail Bars are the latest salons to appear on the high street and if you've ever walked past one when shopping you'll see women sitting for hours while the nail technician transforms their hands. Could you do a basic manicure course so that you get lots of opportunity for a one-to-one with people?

Sarah Stacey (editor of www.beautybible.com) organised a team of therapists for a 'Heaven at Home' party. Stacey and her five friends put on bath robes and sipped strawberry smoothies while the team got to work with a mixture of facials, massages, manicures, pedicures and waxing. They even had a bartender to serve drinks and nibbles and the only fingers they lifted were the ones being manicured.

## health spas

A trip to a health spa is always popular, so consider planning a day away or even longer. Dawn spent a 'top to toe' day with some of her neighbours at a large hotel. While they were sitting in the jacuzzi, chatting, one of the group began to ask Dawn some quite deep questions about her faith. Eight women joined in the conversation, until after half an hour they all emerged from the water looking a little prune-like. So often we believe that sharing our faith will be difficult, yet so often God uses the fun events

[17] **The Female Lifestyle Survey of Great Britain**, commissioned by Top **Sante** magazine, the most comprehensive survey of women's attitudes towards their lives and work ever carried out.

of ordinary living to allow some life-changing conversations to take place. Typing 'health spa' into a search engine such as Google should bring up some venues in your area.

Many women with children will have a lot less to spend on themselves so how about arranging a more domestic version? Even gathering a few friends into your home and giving each other a facial and a manicure would be a welcome offer. It's a great time for a heart to heart. Many beauty therapists and hairdressers report that they often end up as amateur counsellors because clients pour out their troubles as well as their good news when they relax. Play some relaxing music and offer low-fat nibbles and flavoured mineral water. Perhaps you could read some inspirational poetry or a short piece from the Bible while everyone is wearing a face pack. Using a title such as Miracle Morning might open up some interesting opportunities!

Consider having a pamper night, using cosmetics made at home out of store cupboard ingredients, just like Granny used to do it! Cleanse and tone your skin with lavender vinegar, and put on a home-made face mask and pop a slice of cucumber over each eye, lie back and listen to some soothing music and maybe read an inspirational poem to finish.

One of the most humble services one person can do for another is to wash their feet. So give someone a special treat by giving them a refreshing footbath and a pedicure.

### esther

A group of women from the Heaton area of Newcastle attended an Activate event in Gateshead and were inspired by the ideas that seemed to speak right into their desire to serve their community. So after a few 'get togethers' and much prayer, 'Esther' was formed.

Originally the team brought their caring skills into the homes of Christian women who invited their friends along for a pamper evening. Esther quickly 'found favour with all the people' and the team soon had a diary full of bookings. Two years later the Esther group is still committed to the vision, though they have had a few changes of members. They are led by Margaret (a hairdresser) and the team now consists of Sarah (who offers hand massage), Louise (face massage), Karen (make-up), Carol (nails) and Audrey (also a hairdresser). The difference now is that the group has contacted several local welfare projects and the recipients of these beauty treatments are vulnerable women on the margins of society. Some are living on the streets.

Sarah finds that some women struggle at first with her hand massage treatment because of the intimate nature of the touching.

Some of these girls do not have anybody in their lives and they are just not used to being loved. We are very up front about being Christians and we assure them that Jesus loves them. It's up to them to take it further if they want to talk deeply. The heartfelt thanks and comments are very touching. The places we visit include 'The People's Kitchen' which is a place that provides food, clothing and friendship to disadvantaged people in Newcastle and Gateshead. We also visit locations run by the Aquila Housing Association, which help homeless young women in all circumstances. We try to introduce the evening by telling the women about Esther and why we are doing it. Then follows an evening of laughter, sometimes tears but always blessings from the Lord.

The women who we see are usually young and have traumatic histories. However, they never fail to amaze us with how strong and determined they are and how much they have to give. We never 'preach' to them but are open to talking about our faith. Often we find that they are extremely receptive and open to listening about Jesus. Some have even had experience of him personally. For some of these women it may be the first time anyone has touched them in a non-threatening way, or bothered to show them that they are loved.

Once a year we hold an Esther day. This has been run on three occasions and has proved to be extremely successful with some women giving their lives to God following it. It is a day with talks on various women's issues and a Christian speaker. Being part of the team has blessed me in so many ways. Being able to show Jesus' love through our touch or listening skills to these women is such a privilege. We are a close team who pray regularly about Esther and for the Holy Spirit to work through us making a difference to these women. These evenings are about Jesus' love for everyone and Philippians 2:3 tells us, 'Do nothing out of selfish ambition or vain conceit, but in humility consider others better than yourselves.'

## fit to be seen

Going to a keep-fit programme means you can widen your horizons while narrowing your waistline. Join a gym, running club or keep fit class, sign up at Weight-Watchers or visit the health spa. Invite some neighbours to come with you. Often people fancy going but don't want to go alone. Toning up is much more fun with company and you'll make new friends as well as facing the world as a healthier specimen!

Often people go to the gym to meet others. In numerous surveys people stated that they joined a gym to make friends, yet they left because they found that they used the gym without a single person speaking to them. It seems, then, that this would be a perfect opportunity to befriend others and if you love going to the gym why not see this as an opportunity to share God's love in that environment?

Susannah Pilkington is the executive officer for Fit Lives, a small charitable trust, committed to bring the love of Christ to people through fitness venues and activities. 'I used to think evangelism was something scary, to be avoided. I thought it included a soapbox on a street corner, or door knocking and interrupting people eating their tea – aarrgghh!'

Susannah grins. 'Then the penny dropped and I realised that God wanted me to work for him by doing exactly what I enjoyed – down at the gym. It was a huge release and I suddenly understood what Jesus meant by, "My yoke is easy and my burden is light."'

Fit Lives want to recruit co-ordinators who are comfortable in a health club environment and are willing to provide personal support to members and staff. Activities undertaken depend on the skill and fitness of the co-ordinator. Their main task is to provide a friendly face to staff and users of the club, as Fit Lives believe that offering a listening ear in a time-poor society is really valuable and demonstrates a caring attitude. The organisation sets up and runs a small library in each club. They aim to organise occasional lifestyle seminars and video-based courses, offering a Christian perspective on relevant issues such as image, self-worth, time management, business ethics, marriage and parenting. They also offer Alpha courses, which have proved highly successful, with people saying

they would never have gone to their local church to attend the course, but as it was held in their club they felt they could 'give it a go.'

Some health clubs offer dry cleaning, travel agency services, a take-away food service and video libraries. It's not difficult to offer a special deal to encourage people to join. The problem is getting them to stay and, in an attempt to do this, the clubs are striving to meet people's physical, social and spiritual needs. In short, they are trying to create a community where people feel they belong. It's easy to leave an establishment, much harder to leave a group of people. Churches take note.

Realising that relationships are the key, the clubs are often very welcoming to Christians who offer to visit regularly and assist them in this process. They know it makes good business sense! Some health clubs are so appreciative that they run an occasional fund-raising event to assist with the work.

If you enjoy a particular sport, love the sauna or just feel at ease in the club coffee bar environment, then the chances are that you already have a head start by knowing people in your local club. So why not contact Fit Lives to ask about training as a co-ordinator? There is no need to be super-fit or really sporty, the qualities required are social and communication skills, combined with a heart for others and the backing of your church. The time commitment you would need to be prepared to make in each club is eight hours a week.

Take a look at the website www.fitlives.co.uk or contact Susannah Pilkington direct on Tel: 0845 1300 552/Fax: 0870 0111 552 Email: admin@fitlives.co.uk.

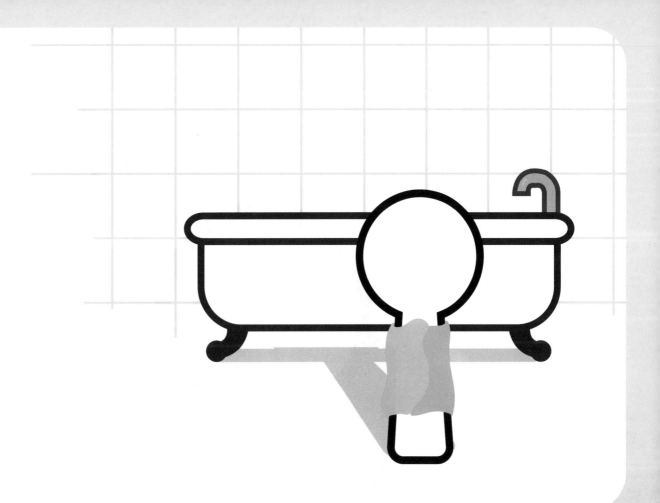

# the study

## working from home

There is a growing trend for people to work from home, and lots of modern houses contain a study. If you can have a break occasionally, why not send brief encouraging e-mails to other busy friends? It's important to keep in touch, or your solitary workplace can be isolating and will dull your creativity.

Drive down almost any motorway in the country and you'll spot signs in fields about the benefits of working from home. Certainly the increased traffic jams make commuting a nightmare and the working day so much longer. The thought of rolling out of bed and into the office is very attractive – especially if you are caring for children, aged parents or pets and require flexibility in your working hours. The advent of Broadband means that many homes have high-speed Internet access allowing home-workers to send and receive e-mails all day long without clogging up the phone line. With the help of a good computer the home office can be as efficient as an office in the average workplace.

There are some pitfalls though. Domestic issues can distract you. Though you can happily put a wash-load in the machine while waiting for the kettle to boil, the ironing pile is always there when you work from home. Though it's great to be able to go to the school carol service or sports day to watch your children taking part, it's inevitable that other parents forget that you are actually working and consider that you are always available to chat or to bail them out when they need someone to help at the Christmas Fair or other such events. It can also be a lonely life without the stimulation of other colleagues to 'bat ideas about', so keep in touch with others as much as possible by phone or email.

On the upside you may be available when people really need you and that is a great feeling. Being there for someone in a crisis can be a huge privilege and will often give you the opportunity to listen and to pray with someone. God uses people who are willing and available. You can be around for the family or take the dog for a walk at lunchtime; a great opportunity to chat with someone as you walk together and good exercise as well.

Home-workers can be part of an online community who aim to support one another. This is a great opportunity as it 'expands your territory' and widens your circle of influence without having to leave the house.

## the workplace

If you work away from home, it could well be that the workplace is the environment where you spend most of your time. When we talk about doing things in the community and reaching out to neighbours we mean it in the widest possible sense, and for you, community and neighbours might mean the people you work with. So consider what you might do to bring God's love into the workplace. If people are interested in faith issues you could run a lunchtime Alpha, but for other colleagues you might need to be a little more creative in order to identify their needs and bring God's love into those situations. Do log on to the LICC website for helpful work-related articles, resources and events – www.licc.org.uk.

Many in the business world have found inspiration from Laurie Beth Jones's book *Jesus CEO*.[19] One director of a large multi-national company said, 'Who would have thought that by living like Jesus you could be successful? This is a book which could be lent or given to a work colleague, who may read it and find that the Bible has a lot to say about the issues they're facing.'

[18] *The Times Book of Quotations* (London: HarperCollins, 2000). [19] Laurie Beth Jones, *Jesus CEO* (New York: Hyperion, 1995).

*each generation seems to identify its own crippling health and social issues and it seems that stress might be one of the top ranking problems of our time.*

For computer users who want to explore the Christian faith anonymously there are excellent websites available that are contemporary, creative and very professionally produced. Try directing your friends to www.church.co.uk or www.rejesus.co.uk

### stress

Each generation seems to identify its own crippling health and social issues and it seems that stress might be one of the top ranking problems of our time. A survey by First Choice Travel revealed that one in five British workers would not take their full holiday entitlement this year. Up to three million full-time workers stay at the office because they are scared of losing their jobs or are simply too busy. Fifty per cent of the female and 40 per cent of the male workforce complain that they are living to work, rather than working to live. It should come as no surprise, therefore, that the Confederation of British Industry (CBI) has estimated that stress and mental health problems cost employers millions of pounds every year in sick pay and lost production.

Social Trends indicate that 70 per cent of women are in paid employment, with more outside the home full-time than part-time employees, and around 20 per cent of women will visit their doctor in any given month with symptoms such as fatigue, sleep problems, irritability and anxiety. The major causes of these stress-related problems are cited as home, family, and career and juggling all three.

Jill and Sue from Kent are both executives with children and busy husbands; their lives are organised like clockwork in order to stay afloat. Up at dawn, they juggle school runs, music lessons, sports, child-minders, housework and shopping with incredible efficiency. When the school rang Jill to say one of her children was ill and needed collecting, the system broke down. Nobody else was available to help and she had three appointments in her diary. 'In the end I had to put off my appointments and rush to the school. On the train I felt so stressed that I thought about opening the door and throwing myself out.'

People who work this hard may not relish spending part of Sunday sitting on a hard pew at church. How can we come alongside them and what would be a convenient time to plan something?

## debt

'In the midst of life we are in debt.' Ethel Mumford [20]

Managing money is something that many people struggle with, but there are those for whom spiralling debt is a crippling issue. It can cause depression, despair, family breakdown or even suicide. Could you help by organising debt counselling in your area? Perhaps arrange a workshop with a retired accountant or bank manager and draw up some helpful guidelines. Or could you think about setting up a Credit Union, a mutual financial co-operative joined by people with a shared common interest, perhaps who work together or live in the same area, which could be managed by volunteers from among the membership? Credit Unions cannot charge more than 1 per cent per month interest on loans, so they are a good way to stop loan sharks getting a grip in your area. For more information contact NACUW on 0845 456 2649 or email them on nacuw@btopenworld.com

## friends reunited

Jane, an ordained minister, logged onto the Friends Reunited website and was delighted to see so many names from her past. She writes

> I remember the friends from primary school more clearly as we had lived and grown up in the same neighbourhood. I chatted with Jackie, Sue, Jennifer and Anne and we arranged to meet up for lunch one Sunday.
>
> I could picture all the girls exactly as they had been at eleven and I was really excited at the prospect of seeing them again. I was the last to arrive as I had to go straight from church, but they promised that they would 'save me a pew'.
> We chatted for hours until we were politely thrown out of the Bistro. Jackie worked with young offenders, and arrived in a posh sports car – courtesy of her second husband! Sue was a teacher; Jenny worked in a Post Office and had grandchildren; Anne was widowed and her son was away in the Army.
>
> It was great to catch up with them and find out about their lives. They were very interested in my ministry and felt that our school must have been 'special' as two of the lads from our year had also been ordained. We keep saying we'll meet up as a group again but so far we've all been too busy. But my husband and I run a singles social group and Anne has joined in a few events with us.
>
> I also exchange emails with a lad from high school who is an agnostic and has a clever scientific mind. We've chatted for hours, and he's also talked with our curate who is an astrophysicist. We've not convinced him yet, but he accepted a Bible from me and I'm hoping he'll argue his way to faith.
>
> Some people criticise Friends Reunited and say that it causes marriage break-ups because a few stories in the press have been blown out of proportion. There may well be people who are looking for their lost youth and getting carried away with

[20] *The Times Book of Quotations* (London: HarperCollins, 2000)

romance. I think there will always be opportunities for sin in life, but I'm sure that, on balance, a website such as this does much more good than harm and can be a wonderful tool for evangelism. It's a perfect forum for sharing lives, values and perspective. Log on and see who is there from your old school, college or workplaces. They might be in desperate need of hearing the gospel.

Log on to www.friendsreunited.co.uk for more details.

Simon is tracing his family tree and through Genes Reunited (part of the Friends Reunited website) has linked up with previously unknown relatives from around the country, giving him another unexpected circle of influence. He says, 'I entered my parents' names and within a short time I had a message back from someone who had the same great-great-grandparents as me. We shared information and began, along with other members of this newly extended family, to correspond with each other.' Log on to www.genesconnected.co.uk.

## photography

As Laura walked across the bridge near her home one evening she was fascinated to see a group of around thirty people, all with tripods, photographing the moon on the river. Always open to new ideas, Laura realised the potential in holding a photographic evening in her home. A recommendation by a friend, soon after, of a young Sheffield photographer called Jodi led Laura to organising a fascinating evening at her home.

About fifty guests, from different backgrounds, crowded into Laura's lounge and watched a delightful visual presentation of lifestyle photography. Beginning with 'tips for amateurs' Jodi showed how to take the most flattering pictures possible, by getting the lighting right and placing the subject at a slight angle for a narrower frame, and how to make people look smaller and taller. This is very helpful advice for amateurs. She then went on to show a sequence of wedding photos. Relating some potentially disastrous episodes at her first wedding shoot kept the guests amused.

As Jodi said

Photography has the ability to record not just how we look but how we feel and where we are in a particular stage of life. Photographs taken in your own environment allow each image to tell a story, reminding you of your home, and your surroundings. The camera gives endless possibilities for creativity and fun and gives me the opportunity to produce works for individuals that they will cherish and value. It's the power that the visual image has to capture a stolen moment of tenderness, and to record people as they are known, and underpinning all this is the truth and inspiration of the Christian message of Jesus – I have found him to be the most singularly inspiring, challenging, gracious and authoritative individual I have ever met. He continues to shape everything I do.

With the increasing popularity of digital cameras, making it ever easier to download our photos onto a computer, could you plan a photographic event locally, either in your home or another suitable venue?

## redundancy/unemployment

Redundancy and unemployment can happen to anyone. They usually come about because a firm has financial problems and needs to make hard decisions, but it's inevitable that the person losing their job will take it personally. This can result in a feeling of rejection and isolation, which can easily spiral into low self-esteem and depression. If you become aware of someone in this position you might be able to help in many ways. First of all, help them to think positively and consider what they would really like to do. Often the thing we most dread can turn out to be the thing which liberates us, and losing a job might be the push we need to find something more stimulating or even more financially rewarding.

Why not see if you can help the person to think objectively about their personal strengths and skills? Perhaps they could use something like the Gallup 'Strengthsfinder'[21] and then construct a new tailored CV, which specifically majors on those strengths. Being accountable to a friend might be the encouragement they need to keep on posting those letters and filling in applications.

You might do this as an individual or alternatively your church or Christian group could offer this as a service in your local community, perhaps even making a room with a computer available to people who don't have that facility at home. Above all, your support will help them to maintain their self-esteem and confidence, which are both crucial when job-hunting.

If you're the person who is out of work, look for opportunities that aren't available to you when you're working. It may be that your circle of influence changes dramatically when you cease to be part of the workforce. If you know of others in the same situation as you, starting a support group might be appropriate. There may be activities in your local area that you can become part of for a time, giving the chance to make new relationships with those you meet in these new situations.

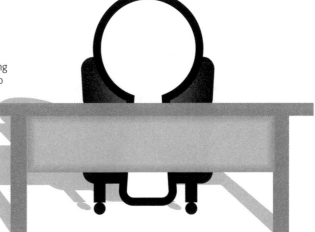

---

[21] Marcus Buckingham and Donald O. Clifton, *Now Discover your strengths* (London: Simon & Schuster, 2001).

# the bedroom

## 'laugh and the world laughs with you; snore and you sleep alone.'

**INSIDE MR ENDERBY, ANTHONY BURGESS**[22]

Your bedroom is the inner sanctum of your home, a place reserved for you and your nearest and dearest.

### clothes

Some people are very happy to turn out their wardrobes every season and make a trip to the charity shop but most of us hoard clothes for years with the intention of slimming into them or finding something to go with random articles of clothing we bought on impulse. Swapping clothes with friends is a great way of acquiring new outfits.

Sarah, a fashion designer in London has regular 'Rag-trade parties'. Friends gather over afternoon tea or evening drinks and barter. She doesn't set any rules but feels it's up to the individual to decide what something is worth and what they are prepared to trade for it. Sometimes they do temporary trades for a weekend so they've got something different to wear for an evening out. She feels it's a great way to spend an afternoon with friends without hitting the credit card, and you get some 'new' clothes into the bargain.

[22] *The Times Book of Quotations* (London: HarperCollins, 2000).

## colour session

Impulse buying is greatly reduced after you've had a colour consultation and a colour session is almost as popular with men as it is with women. The consultant will look at skin tone, eyes and hair colour and help identify the range of colours that suit you best. Often they will supply a swatch of your best colours to assist you when shopping. That way you'll know that anything you buy will match the things already in your wardrobe, and extend the range of your outfits by helping you mix and match what you already have. You might even be tempted to try colours that you've never worn before and discover a whole new look.

Colour Consultation works best in a small group, where people can encourage each other and get some experience of what to look for. These sessions can be fun, deepen your relationship with people and (if you invite a Christian colour consultant) it can be an opportunity for a gentle evangelistic message. They also bring the tantalising potential of a whole new wardrobe. This sounds expensive – but you can always get together with your newly colour-conscious friends and pool resources.

## fashion show

If you want to put on a bigger event, why not consider a fashion show? A local designer outlet might be willing to put this on for you, if you can guarantee an audience and a good location. They'll probably distribute tickets among their customers to boost your numbers. This kind of event draws a large crowd if you do it well. You can easily hire smoke machines, and with a bit of catwalk staging and some music and good lighting it will look very professional. Why not include a glass of champagne and a posh chocolate for an extra treat? Charge an entrance fee to cover costs and give the profits to a local charity for a feel-good factor. One group concluded their fashion show with a five minute talk entitled 'Is God in fashion?'

## sex and relationships

'I know nothing about sex because I was always married.'
Zsa Zsa Gabor [23]

The Bible is very matter-of-fact about sexuality, but in polite Christian circles we mostly avoid talking about it. It's so easy to skirt round or gloss over these issues. But maybe being willing to address them and give a Christian perspective might bring opportunities for evangelism. Somebody once said that minds were like parachutes – they have to be open to be any good! So what is an appropriate response to a generation that already sees Christianity as irrelevant and God as some forbidding killjoy who disapproves of everything they do?

Well, actually sex was God's idea in the first place, wasn't it? Surely when he told Adam and Eve to be fruitful and multiply, this was a Garden of Eden colloquialism for sex. And they certainly took him at his word, as did their descendants after them. The Old Testament is full of people begetting all over the place!

Distinguished Christian psychiatrist Jack Dominian published a book *Let's make love*,[24] subtitled 'the meaning of sexual intercourse' in which he concludes that the church has bound itself into a negative view of this gift of God's good creation. He commends sex as deeply personal and relational, even reflecting the character of God in a mysterious way.

---

[23] *The Times Book of Quotations* (London: HarperCollins, 2000). [24] Jack Dominian, *Let's make love* (Darton, Longman and Todd, 2001).

The front covers of the best-selling magazines which adorn our newsagent's shelves, deal with some aspect of sex in almost every issue. This must lead us to conclude that it's a subject that people are very interested in. What a tragedy that we are surrounded daily with television programmes, art, film and even real-life stories sold to magazines and newspapers, that champion casual sex and pornography yet as Christians we often have so little to say about it and the world assumes our attitudes are negative. Where do people look for sensible answers to their questions about sexuality?

It might seem an adventurous subject to tackle, but if it's done sensibly and with sensitivity it would be a great way of breaking down the myths about Christ, Christians and the church, and could provide a natural forum for the sharing of faith.

## tupperware versus lingerie

Maureen and Gloria have very organised cupboards, thanks to the vast amounts of Tupperware they bought as young mums. Now their daughters, Becky and Sue, have children of their own and live near to each other on a small housing estate, but they have never been invited to a house party selling plastic storage containers. The invitations that they usually receive are for make-up, skincare and lingerie parties.

Becky says:
> We've had lots of invitations to lingerie parties, which feature exotic underwear and sex toys. The girls at work think they are great fun, and up to now we've made tactful excuses not to attend.

Recently we went to an Activate presentation and realised that if we wanted to invite people to our Christian events we might need to get alongside them on their terms first, so we decided to put on a lingerie party ourselves. Being the hosts we had a say on what was demonstrated and so we were able to avoid the more controversial items.

We ended the evening by pointing out that sex was God's idea and it was his provision for us as part of a loving relationship. We've been amazed at the positive response and the frank conversations that have resulted in our 'stepping out'. At least our friends don't think we're prudish now and they seem to appreciate our point of view. We'll have to wait and see if our 'adventure' bears fruit. Our mums didn't really approve but they recognised that we were trying to be creative in our evangelism attempts and we've managed to have a giggle with them about it.

Another way to look at this subject might be to discuss a book such as *Eleven Minutes* by Paulo Coelho[25]. However, be warned. This is a book that contains explicit descriptions of sexual acts and so should be chosen with sensitivity to the other members of the group. A summary of the book and some background information, together with questions for discussion can be found on the Damaris website – www.damaris.org.

Dave and Tara went to see *The Vagina Monologues*, by Eve Ensler[26] and felt that although not all the sketches were edifying, there were some that could form the basis of some excellent discussion material. They have yet to find another Christian couple who have seen these monologues to be able to discuss with them the

[25] Paulo Coelho, *Eleven Minutes* (London: HarperCollins, 2003). See also [26] Eve Ensler, *The Vagina Monologues*,(London: Virago, 2001).

possibilities in using the material for a discussion group. When we consider how explicit a book such as 'Song of Solomon' is, are we in danger of burying our heads in the sand over sex?

## illness

Almost all of us will know at least one person who has suffered from cancer. Eleanor Meade, who lives in North Yorkshire, used her diagnosis of the disease to produce a DVD of interviews with other women who had been through breast cancer. Then, in conjunction with two London hospitals and Rosemary Conley, she put together a series of exercises to use after surgery. It's a great resource to give or lend to a friend. Eleanor has also produced a CD giving her testimony of how she coped with facing her greatest fear. Contact Compassion Productions on 0845 0700 586 for more information.

## divorce

'A divorce is like an amputation; you survive but there's less of you' Margaret Attwood. [27]

With divorce rates soaring, facilitating a Divorce Recovery group in your locality might be a possibility, or just being willing to support a colleague going through divorce may be what's most needed. The London church, Holy Trinity Brompton, have produced a course, 'Recovering from Divorce or Separation' which includes a video set and a course manual. The video includes tips for those running their own course. And further details are available from Alpha resources. The book, *Tracing the Rainbow* (see below) has helpful guidelines on divorce too.

## bereavement

*Tracing the Rainbow* [28] gives practical advice and understanding which will help in coming alongside those who have lost loved ones through death or divorce. It enables us to understand grief in its various forms and the book encourages us to look at how we can help, and hinder, as we try and comfort people.

In cases of divorce and death there can be frequent bouts of loneliness as well as a sense of disconnectedness, and a feeling that the world goes on around us but without us. All too often, people who live alone are never included in invitations to dinner parties or outings. They sometimes feel that they are seen as a threat to other people's relationships. So, many of the activities in this book are ideal for inviting people on their own. Do look at the people around you and be aware of those who live alone.

Take the risk of inviting them to join in; even if they say 'No' they'll probably still appreciate being asked.

[27] **The Times Book of Quotations** (London: HarperCollins, 2000). [28] Pablo Martinez and Ali Hull, **Tracing the Rainbow** (Carlisle: Spring Harvest Publishing Division/Authentic Media, 2004).

# the nursery

## baby massage

Why not invite friends with young babies to baby massage sessions in your lounge? These are becoming very popular and the technique is an easy thing to learn from any good baby book. Alternatively, ask your Health Visitor if she can recommend someone to come and demonstrate it for you.

## dad and me

Toddler groups are popular in every town and village throughout the country, but the dads might like to consider a different take on the traditional group. One mum in Kent asked, 'Why isn't there something like a toddler group for dads to give us a break now and again?' and 'Just Daddy and Me' began. Meeting on one Saturday morning a month, as many as thirty-six dads have attended in a week. It gives mums a break, it's a place where young dads can meet up with others in a similar position and where they may observe their little ones interact with other children in a way they don't usually have the opportunity to do. It's an opportunity to build bridges and friendships through which there's sometimes an opportunity to share the good news of the love of Jesus.

### Diane writes:

In practical terms, the hall set up, is just the same as the Mums and Tots group, with a baby area, craft area, book corner, Wendy House, large apparatus and ride and toy area. Rather than start with a story and song time, because of the fact that some of the Dads stroll in a little late, we have the song time at the end. One dad said, 'I got up at five o'clock this morning to get the two girls ready for this!' Bear in mind they start at ten o'clock! Bless him. The benefits from the group are many. The mums have said how much they appreciate the time, some meet for coffee, some have gone for a facial or just a quiet wander round town without a little person in tow. The dads are also very appreciative of the time. At the end of one song time, one of the dads remarked, 'I've never seen that side of my daughter's character before.' She had just sung a solo into the microphone for us because she knew different words to 'Twinkle, Twinkle...' One mum reported back on a Tuesday that her husband had told her 'I never thought I'd hear myself singing songs about Jesus.'

These Saturdays are really wonderful times. There's a very lively buzz of male conversations, shared play-time between Dad and little one and a safe environment for the children to explore on their own before coming back to check up on Dad. A number of families have begun to attend the family services at the church as a result of this activity.

## Consider this statistic:

- If a child is the first member of the family to become a Christian, approximately 3.5 per cent of families follow.

- If a Mum is the first person of the family to become a Christian, then about 17 per cent of families follow.

- However, if a Dad is the first of the family to become a Christian, a startling 93 per cent of families follow! [29]

[29] *Evangelicals Now*, May 2003.

## babymusic

### Who is it for?

Parents or carers with babies from nine months. Ten adults is fine with a maximum of twelve.

### How do you set it up?

Find a homely and accessible venue with enough room for the group to be in a circle.

Provide a box of props.

Find a suitable tape or CD of songs or a musical person.

Provide suitable refreshments.

### How will people know about it?

Put a notice in the local clinic, NCT groups, inform local community groups and tell your friends.

### Who should lead?

Someone who can sing and does not mind being up front and who has a love of seeing children enjoying themselves.

### What should be in the prop box?

Some toy animals. Anything which matches the subject of a song.

Paint-sprayed cardboard stars.

Scarves and hats.

Drumsticks to tap.

Instruments with different sounds that can be bought or home made.

### What music is best?

A specially recorded CD is available from Ruth Spencer, a music therapist based in Sussex. It's called 'Kids Stuff' and can be ordered by contacting Ruth on ruthaspencer@btinternet.com.

Price £8.50 including postage and packing. Good record shops stock baby songs, lullabies and fun recordings.

### The content?

For very young children the same routine enables them to learn the format and anticipate familiar patterns. New songs can be added from time to time. Add in props, tasks (e.g. ask a named child to find a star for 'Twinkle, Twinkle' etc.), actions, and build up to a dancing section to a lively song. At first the mums do it all with the babies and, as they grow, they achieve the ability to do it themselves.

### The benefits?

An excellent support network; a lot of fun; responsive babies stimulated in movement and music and language and social skills. If you want to talk it through further, then contact: susannahbaker@connectfree.co.uk.

## babysong

Babysong is a similar concept to Babymusic. Julie, the leader says:

'When I first presented the idea of Babysong in a church service, all I asked for was that people in the congregation would pray for the work and for the families that would come. Within a few weeks I was given instruments, offers of help to make the drinks and, most importantly, prayer support. I now have five church members praying for Babysong on a Friday and it gives me peace and confidence that all we do is protected by God and held in his love and that he leads and directs as I prepare and look ahead.'

*Babysong is wonderful and here are a few things that I thank God for as I look back on two years of Babysong:*

○ Being the Creator who makes me creative as I plan the programme.

○ Making it easy to share my faith in the songs and in chats over coffee.

○ The excitement I see in each child's face and body as we sing their name.

○ The way the children use the music day to day at home.

○ A mum saying 'This is the highlight of my week.'

○ Parents getting to know each other and walking up to town for lunch at the end of Babysong.

○ A letter from a mum saying how Babysong has changed their lives and how even dad knows which song to use to soothe a crying baby.

○ The privilege of getting to know families and be able to support them in prayer.

# the children's room

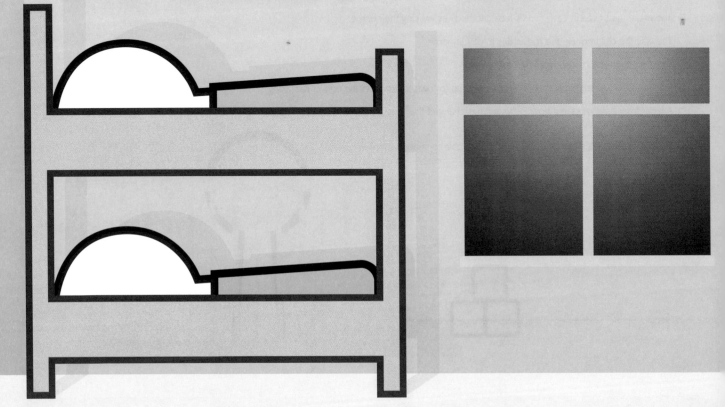

*'we spend the first twelve months of our children's lives teaching them to walk and talk, and the next twelve telling them to sit down and shut up.'* **PHYLLIS DILLER** [30]

Being a parent is tricky, and there's no chance of a dress rehearsal. The encouraging news is that other people around you will be feeling just like you do, so there's no need to struggle in silence. As Sir Peter Ustinov said, 'Parents are the bones on which children sharpen their teeth.'

## parenting groups

Sharing difficulties, failures and successes will help you and help others. So why not consider gathering some other parents around you to start a support group? If the other people are the parents of you children's friends, then so much the better – you can put up a united front over issues when they try out the age-old line, 'Everybody else can, why can't I?'

Parentalk – www.parentalk.co.uk (Tel: 0700 2000 500) and the Family Caring Trust – www.familycaring.co.uk. Tel: 0283 0264174 have both produced excellent materials to help guide your group through six sessions together. Copies of the courses are available from the Activate office to view, prior to purchasing. Take a look at the Parentalk website for lots of helpful advice and articles. The Parentalk Guides cover all aspects of parenting.

Joy and a group of friends began a parenting course, mainly with parents who were not church attenders. They met in a home for six weeks and together used the material provided. The leader just facilitated the group and didn't act as an expert, nor did the other parents look to her for answers. The video clips and parents' handbook provided plenty of discussion material, which gave freedom for lively discussion and disagreement without causing offence. There was time for reflection and relaxation at the end of each session. Joy found the first two courses easy to lead with lots of fun and laughter, particularly during the role-play.

However, a word of caution. Christian parents made up the majority at the third course Joy led and she found this group were far more opinionated and appeared less willing to consider or learn from the experiences of others! Ann had a similar experience with the parenting courses she led. The Christian parents seemed to have less sensitivity to the others in the group than she had expected. While some on the course were struggling with drug, crime and sex-related issues with their young teenagers, the Christians on the course tried to concentrate the discussion on how to ensure their teenager attended church. This appeared a trivial issue to some of the parents compared with the things they were facing. It would be wise to ensure that any Christians attending the group are sensitive to the difficulties that some of the other participants may be dealing with.

[30] *The Times Book of Quotations* (London: HarperCollins, 2000).

## schools

'A teacher affects eternity; he can never tell where his influence stops.' Henry Brookes Adams 1838-1918 [31]

A great many wars are held in the classroom. As students recognise the limits of the teacher's authority, and discipline levels are eroded, more and more teachers are abandoning the profession, and those who do stay can often feel demoralised. Now, more than ever, teachers need the support of parents to affirm them. Parents need to join the PTA and keep in constant touch with the establishment where children spend most of their weekdays, and to fund-raise to ensure that the children have access to the best possible facilities.

School governors come from all walks of life; it's good to have a diverse mix and parents are particularly welcome. If your children are still at school, joining the PTA is a good move. You get to know the teachers personally which makes them more approachable and more accessible should a problem occur. It means that you find out about events at the planning stage, rather than two days after the event when you find a screwed up newsletter in a blazer pocket when you're washing it.

You can also give your practical support to the school. Even if your children don't attend it, the school will still be glad of some help and will value your contribution. Events need organisers, marshals, someone to make refreshments or take tickets at the door. Fund-raising is often a big issue in schools and PTA events provide much needed resources.

All these events will bring you into contact with new people with a shared interest. You'll also get to know children your own are mixing with, and this will give you an insight into what makes your children tick. Maybe their friends will recognise you as a sympathetic ear and a sounding board when they struggle with teenage angst and their own parents 'just don't understand'.

Some Christian organisations have excellent links with schools and regularly have opportunities for Christians to go in and chat with pupils. Volunteers are asked to go into classrooms for pre-arranged sessions to share their experiences of being a Christian in their chosen field of work. Contact the Spire Trust – Tel. 01491 839627 or Scripture Union – Tel. 01908 856000 or log on to www.scripture.org.uk for further information.

'Children today are tyrants. They contradict their parents, gobble their food and tyrannise their teachers.' Socrates 469 BC - 399 BC. [32]

## mothers and daughters

Jo writes:
> My daughter and her classmates turned sixteen this year and the end of term is a disorganised affair, with the girls not really getting together again as a form after their exams are completed. I organised a 'Mothers and Daughters' event at a local restaurant, and held it in March, just before revision fever took hold.
>
> I sent out an invitation stating clearly that the object of the meal was to say encouraging things about our daughters before their exams. I suggested there would be a prize for the most effusive

[31] *The Times Book of Quotations* (London: HarperCollins, 2000).

[32] *The Times Book of Quotations* (London: HarperCollins, 2000).

and embarrassing mum! Thirty mothers and daughters responded and paid a deposit, so we were on! By the time the meal finished on the evening of the event, the restaurant was really noisy so I commandeered a quieter part of the restaurant and we all moved upstairs.

I'd intended to go first, to encourage other mums to follow suit, but my one Christian co-worker got in first. We'd not had any prior discussion, and it was just marvellous to have her alongside. This fantastic lady was not only raising her own daughter, but had been looking after another school friend for a year whose own family had returned to Germany. As she read a poem from the mum in Germany the girls began to weep. Then she blessed her own daughter, and said how Jesus had made all the difference in their lives. So, now I'm ready to go second, but the next mum who pops up overtakes me. She's just had chemotherapy for breast cancer and is wearing a wig. It's very poignant, because we all know what a tough year this lovely family has had, and off she goes, singing the praises of her youngest daughter and blessing the socks off her. We're all sobbing now, because it's so real and not stage-managed in any way. Next comes a Jewish mum. Then another. I finally get my turn, but there's very little for me to say that the others haven't said.

Finally, one of the girls stood up. She had come without her mum and was clearly very moved. She was a Hindu. 'Since the moment we got upstairs, I have been feeling all trembly,' she said. 'I think this evening has been wonderful and I want to thank you very much for organising it.'

So that was that! The evening exceeded my wildest dreams. We've got three sons to get through before my final daughter sits her GCSE's, so the next evening should be 'Dads and Lads', but that's another story.

An idea such as this gives the opportunity for an annual reunion, allowing you to keep in touch with those you've made an initial contact with.

# the spare bedroom

If you have a spare room in your house, would you be willing to share it from time to time?

*'and mighty proud I am (and ought to be thankful to God almighty) that I am able to have a spare bed for my friends.'*

THE DIARY OF SAMUEL PEPYS. [32]

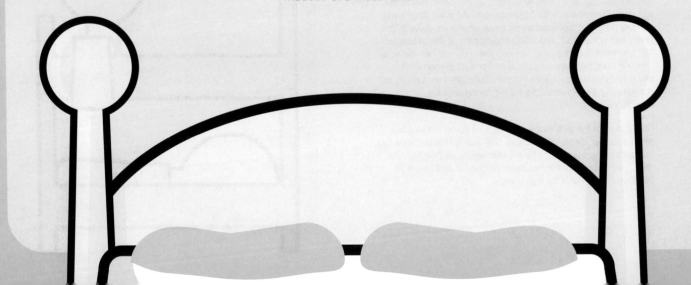

## overseas students

Overseas students are often not able to go home in the holidays because the cost of the airfare is prohibitive. This makes them vulnerable and lonely, particularly at Christmas, when the rest of Britain is clearly celebrating. The organisation 'Host' can link you up with a lonely student who would be grateful to stay within a family home over the holidays. Small acts of kindness cost us very little and can enrich our lives and widen our own horizons, and they are appreciated so much by the recipients. Contact Host on www.hostuk.org.uk or Telephone 020 7254 3039.

## fostering

Thousands of vulnerable children are in care in this country, desperately in need of loving homes. Is this something you could consider? There are lots of fostering agencies around the country that will be happy to chat informally about what's involved, or contact your local Social Services Fostering Department. More information from the British Association for Fostering and Adoption at www.baaf.org.uk (Tel: 020 7593 2000) or Adoption UK at www.adoption.org.uk or (Tel: 01295 752240).

## tesol

Jane spent a week on an introductory TESOL course (Teaching English to Speakers of Other Languages) and found it so stimulating, and that it offered so many opportunities for getting alongside people, that she went on to take the full five-week course. She now helps in a unit in an inner-city area where refugees and asylum seekers go to learn English. She finds it a privilege to get to know the students and to show love and patience, sitting alongside them week after week as they struggle with our alphabet, verbs, tenses and pronunciation. There are occasionally opportunities to say something specifically Christian but that's not the aim of the lessons. Jane says, 'There are more opportunities when we celebrate Christmas or Easter and can invite them to special events.'

Our university towns and cities have increasing numbers of overseas students keen to understand the British way of life, to visit our homes and to know what Christians believe. One student expressed a hope that she would make friends with English people and be invited into their homes but was told by her tutor that this was extremely unlikely, as English people didn't invite foreigners into their homes.

Jane and her husband have hosted a number of groups in their home where international students come for supper and then study the Bible for an hour. Several students have asked to attend church with them, and some have become Christians. 'I've felt as if God has been saying "Jane, I'm working here. Would you like to come and join me?" What a privilege! Yes, the world is on my doorstep – and yours. This is God's world and he is at work in it.'

## refugees and asylum seekers

One hundred miles away, in another urban area, Jean was teaching English to Asian women when a variety of asylum seekers began attending her classes. She recognised that they all had in common a sense of shock, bereavement and isolation, and she began inviting them home for meals.

[33] Peter Drucker, *Managing for the future – the 1990s and beyond* (Middlesex: Penguin, 1992).

One of the men seemed vague, lacking in confidence and a bit scruffy and I assumed he was semi-literate. It took several weeks and some mutual hospitality to recognise that this man was intelligent, cultured and charming. He was an engineering graduate, spoke fluent Russian and two Afghan languages and had been brought up in a wealthy family.

I have learnt to see past first impressions. Most of the refugees I meet are highly intelligent with sophisticated political opinions and a sense of justice. I have also come to see that these are family men and women who have fled from death and who ache to see and hold their children, parents and wives. Their existence is lonely and confused. Often their sleep is tormented by nightmares. England is a cold and inhospitable place and we locals often fail to see the depth of their pain.

It's worth getting to know the asylum seekers in the local area. Their problems may almost overwhelm us but they value the genuine welcome that comes when we invite them into our homes for a meal. Several churches have now started drop-in sessions, befriending and offering practical help and hospitality. If there are asylum seekers housed in your community why not consider this as part of your outreach?

'When an alien lives with you in your land, do not ill-treat him. The alien living with you must be treated as one of your native-born. Love him as yourself, for you were aliens in Egypt. I am the LORD your God.' (Lev. 19:33,34)

## scrapbooking

Scrapbooking is a very simple idea which appeals to all ages. Men, women, children from around six years of age, grandparents and those in residential homes and hospices all enjoy this form of creativity. The photographs we take over the years are priceless but in reality are often left in a box and forgotten. Scrapbooking encourages us to make the most of the pictures we take, making a record of our story to pass on to our families and friends, recording the things that are important to us.

Rebecca runs evening workshops and classes in her home, inviting people to come and try their own first page. If they want to continue they come back each month and new relationships are built. One woman, receiving chemotherapy treatment herself, has set up a group for others she met at the hospital, to help them produce something meaningful and lasting for their families.

The opportunities are numerous. Work colleagues, friends, neighbours, relatives, those who grieve, those who want to write a life journal and those who need some time out of a busy life, can all be reached. The conversations which take place while the people are working on their pages provide great opportunities to make new relationships.

## crafts and hobbies

Crafts are making a comeback, so why not while away the winter nights with a small group who are knitting, quilting or stitching. You could buy each other's efforts as presents, or learn new skills from each other. There are numerous books available in the library – so there's no excuse for idle hands.

*those who grieve, those who want to write a life journal and those who need some time out of a busy life, can all be reached.*

Often the spare room is the place where materials are stored for hobbies. You might keep a sewing or knitting machine in there, or embroidery and tapestry yarns. You might keep glue and ribbons for card-making or scrapbooking. Or your spare room might be the place you go to do jigsaws or build models. With all these things you can choose to be solitary or inclusive. Do them alone, or as part of a small group. If you do share with others this gives lots of opportunities to share your perspective on life.

## knitting

With celebrities such as Geri Halliwell and Julia Roberts publicly declaring their devotion to the humble art of knit one, purl one, the recent success of knitting clubs shouldn't surprise us. (Take a look at www.castoff.info for more details.). With all the publicity about stress amongst women, knitting is seen as a great stress reliever. One devotee said 'You get into a kind of rhythm which I find relaxing.' One London based knitting group feels knitting is a great icebreaker – it's not unusual to find artists, office workers and city professionals clicking side by side and the conversations which then ensue have all sorts of possibilities.

The Activate office has some knitting patterns; one is for a child's jumper, which needs very little sewing up and the other is for a small teddy that will be sent off in his own little drawstring bag. Both these items are for children in war-torn countries who have lost everything. The knitted items are transported free of charge along with other shipments of humanitarian aid. Could you rally a group to knit Teddies for Tragedy or make small drawstring bags to send the teddies in? Contact the Activate office (Tel: 01384 370775) for copies of the patterns and details of where to send the finished items.

## pottery painting

Pottery painting is a new craze in London. There are three Pottery Cafés where you can meet a group for tea and biscuits or throw a party. Everything is provided for your group to decorate purpose-made pots – paint, sponges, aprons and pottery. Ring 020 8744 3000 or visit www.pottery-cafe.com. Readers in the north can try the Naked Plate Company in Accrington, Lancashire. They have a mobile kiln and can come out to organised parties, www.thenakedplate.com.

# the attic

## spring

Spring is a time for a new start, so have a grand clear-out of your attic, shed, garage and junk room. If you're going to the local tip with a trailer, why not mention it to a neighbour and offer to take their junk. But before you drive off with your stuff ... is there anything you might give to the local charity shop? Can you have a stand at a car boot sale and have some Christian leaflets for people to pick up at your stall? Some groups have set up at Easter car boot sales, giving away Hot Cross buns with an appropriate booklet.

You can always turn your spring cleaning into a discussion topic. Gather some friends for supper and ask them which five items they would rescue if they had to leave their homes in a hurry. Discuss how you would rate your homes on the clutter scale and why we hang onto things we don't really need. End by pondering what important things we need to make room for in our lives.

## summer

Summer seems to be such a short season in Britain. No sooner have we dug out our garden chairs and parasols than they are being stored away again. So plan ahead for the summer. Set aside some Saturdays to have a barbecue or garden party and invite the neighbours. If you are worried about rain, why not invest in a canvas cover or a party marquee? There are a good range of inexpensive ones at garden centres and DIY stores. Plan a treasure hunt to keep any children amused, with a series of clues leading to some sweetsn.

[24] *The Times Book of Quotations* (London: HarperCollins, 2000).

## autumn/bonfire night

A good time to clear out your loft is around bonfire night when you can invite all your neighbours round for the ritual burning of all your old broken furniture. There's something about a fire that draws people together. For more details see The garden section.

## winter

Throughout January, local theatres will be putting on their pantomimes and it can be great fun to let out your 'inner child' with a few friends. Take along some children if you must – but you'd be surprised at how many adults enjoy the sheer escapism of a silly pantomime. Make a night of it with supper afterwards. If you want something more sophisticated why not go to the ballet or the opera? If you organise a group booking you can often get cheaper tickets or a free one to treat a friend. If you live in the North West try www.englandsnorthwest.com. Your local theatres may well have their own websites.

If the much longed-for snow arrives, why not go sledging? You can buy a posh designer sledge or a cheaper plastic one. Country dwellers have even discovered that fertiliser bags take you down the hill at fantastic speed but don't protect you from rocks and big stones! It's great fun for children and adults alike. In these days of global warming, skating on rivers and lakes is a risky occupation, but you could try some seasonal fun at the ice rink. Some cities now set up open-air rinks for the winter. Have a giggle watching first-timers attempt their first wobbly steps in the boots. But do wrap up warmly and protect yourself with extra padding. This can be a wonderful ice-breaker (no pun intended) for a community group. If you are more adventurous you could try skiing or snowboarding. There are seventy dry-snow centres in the UK so there should be one near you.

## advent

There are two specific seasons in the church calendar that are set aside for reflection. One is Lent, which is for personal prayer and fasting, and the other is Advent – a time when the church collectively is meant to prepare for the second coming of Christ.

Bishop William Temple said that the church was the only society on earth that existed for the benefit of those who are not members. How easily we forget those wise words in our battles to shape our services and church activities to suit ourselves.

The church is made up of individuals and we can use the season of advent to consider our own impact on our immediate community. As we make personal preparation to celebrate Christmas, how can we share this time and draw neighbours and friends in?

The loft is probably the home for boxes of swags and baubles and other Christmas decorations. As you consider how you might celebrate Christmas, do think about those for whom this is the loneliest time of the year. Festivities seem to go on indefinitely if you're not a part of them and, in the run-up to Christmas, the television is full of adverts depicting happy families.

Christmas is one of the busiest times of year for The Samaritans, as people are most acutely aware of their loneliness and isolation. Over 30 per cent of households in Britain now comprise of one person, many of whom have no close family or friends to celebrate with. Christmas is a perfect time for getting people together. Can you have an open house this Christmas and invite lonely neighbours and acquaintances to share food? Don't feel you have to supply it all, people prefer to contribute. If you've got people from other countries living locally why not ask them to bring some traditional food from their homeland. You'll be amazed at how enriched your celebrations will be and the novelty and informality takes away all the pressure of everything having to be just right.

Even the food preparation can be a great community thing, peeling carrots and shelling peas together is a good way to relax and get to know each other. By the time the food is ready to eat, the ice will be well and truly broken. Tell stories, maybe get everyone to share childhood Christmas memories, good or bad, and ask what they would most like to have in their stocking this year.

Tearfund produce three Christmas resource packs for £4.95 each (visit the Tearfund website at www.tearfund.org). Contact the Activate office for an Activate Christmas Pack (£3.00 + 50p p & p) containing a host of Christmas ideas (Tel: 01384 370775).

## unusual christmas gifts

What will you buy for the person who has everything? If you want a perfect opportunity to share good news this Christmas, then instead of trailing round the shops for the same old bath products, why not host a party giving alternative ideas for Christmas presents?

World Vision has produced the Alternative Gift catalogue, which, it says, puts the fun back into giving. It's a quick and easy way of buying a unique gift while giving someone in another country a brighter future. It's packed with gloriously original gifts to suit every budget, from a flock of sheep to a vegetable garden. Every gift will support a child, family or community in the developing world, helping someone on their journey out of poverty.

And it's not only for Christmas. When friends inquired what they wanted for their Silver Wedding Anniversary, Andy and Sarah sent them a catalogue from World Vision and instead of gifts they received cards, confirming that an emergency water kit, two chickens, apple trees and a herd of goats had been sent overseas to those who had very little. In addition, two cataract operations were performed and several children were immunised. This idea can be used for birthdays too. Contact World Vision on www.greatgifts.org or ring 0845 600 6446. World Vision also produces special resources for Christmas, Harvest, young people and home groups.

Organisations such as Christian Relief Uganda (CRU) also offer the opportunity to send gifts abroad on behalf of friends, and will send you a certificate to give to people so that they are aware of the gesture. CRU support a small community which includes an orphanage called Maria's Care, a school and an initiative to set young people up in small businesses to enable them to be self-supporting after leaving the school. You can send money to purchase a goat, pig or hens; agricultural seeds or trees; an item for the school or church; or a starter pack for young people setting up their own home.

Friends are usually amazed and thrilled by this unusual gesture and there is a feel-good factor in being part of a scheme such as this. Some groups of Christians have stopped giving cards to each other; instead they all sign a greeting in one large card and the money they save goes to charity. For CRU information contact Rhona Marshall on 01625 618319.

## new year resolutions
Our challenge to you, whatever time of year you read this, is to attempt to come alongside at least one new person this year, so that you can bless them, spend time with them, meet their needs and then proclaim the gospel to them (Lk.10). 'Each One Reach One' is the resolution we are asking you to consider. Write it on a post-it note and stick it by your telephone. ~

## slimming club
A great crowd puller after festive over-indulgence is a local slimming club. Most people don't like going alone but might be willing to go in a group. You might need to be sensitive about inviting people to this! You can swap recipes and encourage each other to shed those extra pounds before the spring. As an extra treat you could organise trips to a health club or spa. Then, when you've lost weight, a shopping trip might be in order. The things we endure for evangelism! Before you go shopping you might like to have a colour consultation session.

## lent
February brings another opportunity for bringing out what you've got in the house. Shrove Tuesday is traditionally the time for using up all your store-cupboard perishables before the Lenten fast begins. Why not throw a Pancake party for your neighbours and friends? You'll need plenty of milk and some eggs and flour, but consider asking each person to bring an unusual filling, enough for everyone to sample.

## easter
Why not consider some Easter activities with friends? You could throw a chocolate party, do Easter crafts, or arrange an egg rolling and Easter egg hunt for families. For all your chocoholic friends why not organise a chocolate party? See Chocolate party guidelines under 'The kitchen'. Activate has an Easter Pack containing lots more ideas, available from the office – Tel: 01384 370775.

Brainstorm with others and create ideas for other special events such as Valentine's Day, Mother's Day and Father's Day.

the
granny flat

*people view retirement in a variety of ways – for some it is a longed-for freedom, for others it threatens boredom, inertia and a feeling of being on the scrap heap.*

## retirement

People view retirement in a variety of ways – for some it is a longed-for freedom, for others it threatens boredom, inertia and a feeling of being on the scrap heap. Many people fear ageing.

The four stages of life are often categorised by organisations working with the elderly as follows:

**First Age:** dependence, socialisation, immaturity, education (childhood).

**Second Age:** independence, maturity, responsibility (possibly raising children), earning.

**Third Age:** personal fulfilment, active independence.

**Fourth Age:** dependence and dignity.

There are currently around twelve million British people in the Third and Fourth ages. This is a great mission field. Older people are now finding a new freedom as they retire from work and look for new pastimes – things they really want to do now they are free from the obligations and demands of employment and bringing up children. Many use their time creatively and find new skills in painting or other crafts. Others take advantage of low season holidays or preferential rates at leisure facilities. And for those who prefer to flex their intellectual muscles there are courses available with the University of the Third Age.

No need to rush off to work or worry about the potentially negative impact on your career. Our increased longevity has given us a completely new map of life – but often the focus is on the problem of ageing while the enormous potential of the Third Age is not always recognised.

Those over sixty possess competence and availability, a precious combination, especially in relation to Christian ministry. It can be a great time for making new friends, getting to know your neighbours and sharing your faith with others in a relaxed way. It can be the best time of your life, as Roberts Browning predicted in his poem 'Grow old along with me, the best is yet to be'.

Many people who share this sentiment are taking opportunities for early retirement. Sports personalities are forced to retire early, which is great if you've earned enough in a short career to be comfortable throughout your life, especially if you've been

# 'am I too old at seventy-three to come and join one of your Eden teams?'

particularly successful in your chosen field. Muhammad Ali famously said on announcing his retirement: 'I want to get out with my greatness intact.'

While modesty prevents most of us from agreeing with Ali's comment, there is something to be said for quitting while you're ahead. Some retired people take on the responsibility for looking after grandchildren while their parents are at work. Again, this gives opportunity to get alongside others and share our faith. Relationships can be struck at the school gate, toddler groups, and swimming or dancing lessons. As we bring our collective experience into parenting groups it's a good way of brushing up on 'rusty' parenting skills.

Do you have a 'Caleb' attitude to retirement? He couldn't wait to get to the Promised Land. He'd caught a glimpse of this highland paradise on earth while on a preliminary survey forty-five years previously and then, at last he was about to go in and enjoy its delights, despite being eighty-five years old. It can be easy to slip into the attitude of 'leaving it to the younger ones' yet there are so many opportunities to make a difference, whatever our age.

## hazel's story

As a fifteen-year-old, recuperating from an illness, Hazel felt God's call to the mountainous regions of China. Forty years later she had the chance to 'spy out the land' when she completed a one hundred kilometre sponsored walk along the Great Wall of China in 1999 for the Children's Society. She subsequently joined a short-term team working in an orphanage in China in 2002 and since then has spent several months in China using her skills as a paediatric physiotherapist. More recently she's spent six weeks in Morocco setting up day centres for children with physical handicaps. Her accounts of her travels and the ways God is using her are inspiring, challenging and at times quite scary, yet she loves it all, and is making a real difference.

## doris' story

Doris was seventy-four years old and lived in sheltered accommodation. 'I've invited my neighbours to church events but they're not interested; I've no money and I feel I can't do anything for God.' A little probing revealed that Doris spent much of her time knitting and often sat alone at home engaged in this craft. And so, it seems, did some of her neighbours. Doris saw the potential for making real friendships with the other residents by inviting them for afternoon tea each week, and spending the time knitting together. They use patterns provided by 'Teddies for Tragedy' and knit teddies and jumpers which are then sent to children in war-torn countries. Further details from the Activate office (Tel: 01384 370775).

## liza's story

Fiona Castle's older sister, Liza, at the age of seventy-three, sold her home, left her friends and moved to inner city Manchester to work on the Eden Project. This is her story.

When my husband died seven years ago, I looked at my life and said to the Lord, 'Lord, I am tired of the comfort zone, I want to be at the 'coal face'. I am willing to sell up and move into the slums of Manchester, Liverpool, London or wherever, but I must hear from you exactly the place of your choosing.

That time came in the summer of 2002. I heard a talk by Andy Hawthorne from the 'Message Trust', a Christian outreach to young people in the deprived areas of Manchester, who were running wild on the streets learning to become 'prison fodder'. As Andy spoke all my 'spiritual bells' began to ring, and when he called for volunteers, willing to give up at least seven years of their lives to live and work in those difficult areas, I wondered if this was what I was waiting for.

Eventually I rang The Message and asked, 'Am I too old at seventy-three to come and join one of your Eden teams?' The response quickly came, 'No, we need grannies and mums!'

I was assigned to Eden Harpurhey, a difficult district two and a half miles from the centre of Manchester. Intercessors had been praying for eighteen years for Christians to move into Harpurhey, and had been given several confirming prophecies that this area would be restored and people would come crowding into the church to find the love of Father God through Jesus.

Culture shock? Yes, but I love it, and I love the people, but am deeply saddened by the plight of so many. Parents who have had God's love so badly misrepresented to them that they, in turn, inflicted their hurts and anger on their own children. People seek love or fulfilment in drink, drugs, sex and vandalism, leaving their children without boundaries and without love. Gang culture becomes their natural environment and violence the norm. How can you love if you have never been given love? How can you succeed if you have never been affirmed and have no self worth? Hopelessness prevails.

Samantha came to an Alpha course I was asked to lead, an alcoholic for many years with seven children living in a back-to-back two-bedroom house. On that first day she wanted to be different and invited Jesus into her life to change it. Going through exhausting withdrawal symptoms, prayer was given, asking God to enable her to become an overcomer. From that moment she was healed of her alcoholism. Such was the change in her that family and friends wanted to know about 'this Christianity.' Samantha has been discipled well by her Christian neighbour and began to give her family strong loving boundaries. Consequently the children became quieter and happier. The youngest changed so much, his teachers were

# we don't have to be young, fit and well to share our faith with others

asking what had transformed him so dramatically. Samantha now holds meetings regularly in her home where family and friends can ask questions and learn about Jesus. The wonderful harvest from this one seed, sown in the ground with love and prayers, continues to grow and spread.

## norman's story – a witness in wine

We don't have to be young, fit and well to share our faith with others. Norman Richardson is in his seventies and spent two lengthy sessions in hospital having replacement hip joints. Although he took every opportunity to chat with people and share his faith during his stay, he was determined to deliver a memorable departing shot...

As my time to be discharged from hospital approached, I was wrestling with the problem of how I could thank the orthopaedic team for their care and kindness in a way that might be acceptable to them and yet a witness to my own faith in Jesus. After rejecting a few ideas I settled on a bottle of wine; there had been a time years ago when I came across an Italian wine called Lacryma Christ, which literally means 'Tears of Christ'. As I thought about this name I could see that

I could do a short write-up, linking compassionate nursing with the compassion shown for people by the Lord himself. From one point of view nursing must bring difficult experiences because of the intense suffering of the patient. At such times nurses must cry with the patient in empathy, just as Jesus does with us.

From another point of view, nursing staff in their own lives must, from time to time, feel the need for someone to cry with them for their own trials. No doubt the promise Jesus made to be with us when we call to him will hold good for each of us. As Hebrews 4:15 says, 'He is able to sympathise with us in our weakness'. I felt this was an idea given to me by the Lord, and the following day asked my son to see if he could find a wine importer who could supply the 'Lacryma Christi'. The Internet soon supplied the answer, and a case of wine was delivered to my home within four days. My son's computer skills provided most attractive 'Thank You' cards, with a message explaining why this particular wine had been chosen. Each bottle was provided with a 'collar', carrying an explanation to the recipient. The following is the explanatory text, and my prayers go with it that Jesus will be able to make a connection in his time.

### lacryma christi – an italian wine.

This wine comes with a big thank you for all the surgical and nursing skills experienced during two hip-replacement operations over a 15-month period, in the John Charnley Unit. I have chosen this particular wine because of its unusual name 'Tears of Christ.'

First, it's a smooth wine of gentle remembrance. Perhaps it will bring to your mind people whom you have treated in the past whose suffering brought you close to tears. The 'Tears of Christ' seem especially appropriate to celebrate these people you have helped.

Second, it's an empathic and comforting wine. Perhaps you remember your own hard times when you needed someone to share your difficulties or pain. As you drink the wine then, be thankful to Jesus Christ who, even if you did not know it, shed His tears with you.

I offer this gift and these thoughts because of my own experience of finding strength and comfort in the tears of the real Christ, as I have learnt of Him so vividly in the Bible.

With very best wishes and many thanks
Norman Richardson

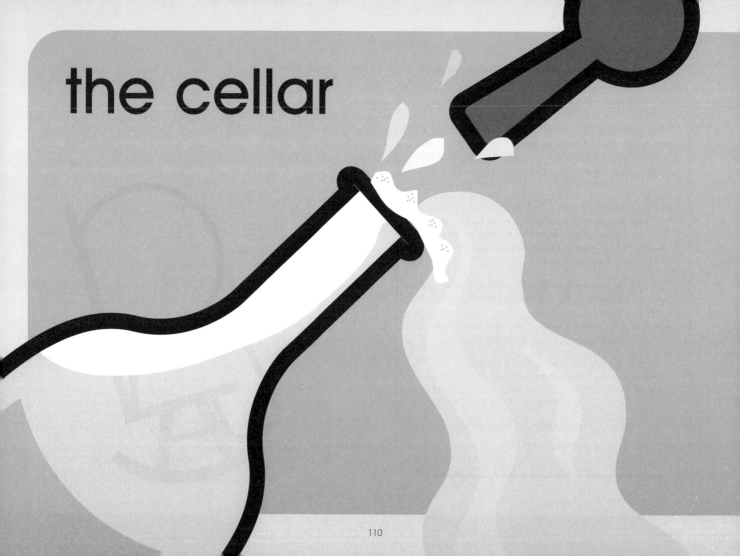

the cellar

# 'when I am in the cellar of affliction I look for the Lord's choicest wines' SAMUEL RUTHERFORD

## a champagne moment

Wine tasting or cheese and wine evenings have been regularly used in an informal setting as a way of getting people together so why not try champagne? When is the right time to have a champagne moment? Many people appeared to have one at the Good Food Show in Birmingham recently, surrounded by Jamie Oliver, Gordon Ramsay and Ainsley Harriot!

A recent evening held in Chester started with an informal talk on the history of champagne and its production. A champagne tasting event may not be for everyone so it is probably helpful to do your homework first. Champagne is expensive and viewed as a treat so you may wish to combine the event with another activity. How could you develop this idea to suit your group of friends?

- A champagne breakfast with a speaker linked to the theme of celebration.
- A small personal event with a blind tasting of a limited range of champagnes.
- Strawberries and champagne linked to Wimbledon.
- Cookery with champagne or cookery involving foods that compliment champagne.

If you feel this may be something you could explore, there's more information available on www.champagneshop.co.uk or ring The Champagne Shop on 0870 013 0105.

## reach-a-street

For the team who visit the same twenty-five houses each week Reach-a-Street has become more than a method or a project, it's a way of life. It's not a way of getting people into the church but a way of serving and blessing people through the demonstration of faith. The purpose is to offer three jobs: gardening, taking items to the tip and car washing. With the same adult Christian leading the team, they can help take the inevitable opportunities to share their faith and offer prayer where appropriate. As time goes on and the relationships develop the team can become almost a counselling service, maybe run personal errands or meet any number of needs for the residents.

'We started reaching out this way after many years of feeling like salesmen when doing evangelism,' says David, the team leader. 'Through a series of events we got to know a pastor from the Dream Center, Los Angeles. We were so convicted by the way they were seeing lives changed that we decided to visit them. We saw a ministry called Adopt-a-Block. Teams of people were literally adopting blocks of houses and giving their lives for them in practical, relational and spiritual ways. It just seemed we had found what we were looking for – a way of really loving people. We felt we could adapt this to the British way of life in a way that felt natural to us.

'Society is changing. It is transient which means many do not even know their neighbours. Trust is diminishing rapidly causing many to feel self-sufficient. Reach-a-Street members come humbly into this situation offering trust, local friendships and stability. Surprisingly, we find nearly all the residents open to offers of help, prayer and friendship – they kind of feel this is what the church should really be doing.

'"How are you today, Simon?" I asked. "Not very well. My wife died in hospital and was buried yesterday." I was stunned. Within minutes we were crying and praying together. Simon's world had slowly fallen apart over the years. After the "high" of his son winning a silver medal in the Olympics to the "low" of his later suicide, this widower lives in a one-bedroom maisonette with his other son, who is mentally retarded. He can't bear to go back to his overgrown home where the suicide took place.

'Reach-a-Street is built on the foundations of love and faithfulness. The world does not expect us to be unconditional towards them as they may have an alternate lifestyle or different beliefs. They are surprised that we are faithful, with some initially expecting us to fizzle out after a few months. But how else can we convince them of God's unconditional love, of a faithful, covenant love that never fails?

We have had our own spiritual lives deepened dramatically throughout the last five years whilst doing Reach-a-Street. We are discovering that getting close to people means getting close to God. Our hearts have been tested and our faith has been stretched as we are faced with people who are different to us and need miracles.'

David and Sam Hazeldine can be contacted via the Goldhill Baptist Church website – www.goldhill.org. They have a manual to help you set up Reach-a-Street. They also travel to churches giving a video presentation, teaching on the principles of Reach-a-Street and sharing testimonies.

## community prayer

At an event in Devon, a woman told how prayer was transforming her area. The streets around the church are divided up and each is visited on a regular basis, usually three monthly. During week one the team visits each home in the street and explains that the following week the road will be the focus of prayer. Does the household have anything they'd like the church to pray for? Rarely is the door slammed in the faces of the team, as the residents are invariably facing some crisis from illness to redundancy. When the team returns three months later, there are always answers to prayer, which occurred during the week that particular road was prayed for. And the group has found that being willing to pray for a road means that at times they need to put feet on their prayers and become more involved with some of the families.

# we are discovering that getting close to people means getting close to God

## sport

For many people, joining their local running, football, swimming or tennis club can be a great way of meeting new people and building up relationships with them. Think of a sport you've always wanted to develop your skills in and find out what's already available in your area, and join in. Sometimes it's more effective to become involved in something already organised than to start something new.

Christians in Sport have a variety of resources and run one, five and nine-day courses to help Christians use sporting activities to share God's love. Take a look at their website for more ideas and information – www.christiansinsport.org.uk.

# the conservatory

The Conservatory is often the room where we can sit, reflect on life and take stock of our lives. Take a quiet few minutes to look at your own life by considering the questions below. Imagine that one day, long after you have passed away, one of your great-grandchildren asks about you and your life.

- How would you want to be remembered and described? Write a summary of your life, as you would like it to be related to your great-grandchild.

- Be sure to include a description of your values and your personal characteristics. Put this to one side for a couple of days and then come back to it. Think not only about what you included in your summary but also what you left out.

- Are there activities that take up a great deal of your time that weren't included?

- Why did you leave them out?

- What changes could you make in your life so that the summary would be an accurate picture of your life?

Sharing the responses to these questions with others in a group could be helpful to everyone. It's the sort of exercise a life coach might recommend, to help someone wanting to move on in their lives.

We've already seen that people today are actively searching for a meaning to life and, whereas years ago they may have looked to the church for the answers, today they are reading an increasing number of self-help books and flocking to life coaches to help them sort out their lives and fulfil their potential. This might be because many Christians can hear hundreds of sermons, Sunday after Sunday yet still have no real idea of how to relate what they hear on a Sunday to their everyday lives during the rest of the week.

The increasing popularity of self-help books emphasise the interest many people having in improving their lives. Consider the following

A life coach focuses on the resources you have now, focuses on what's possible for you; says, what you are is OK but can be improved on. A life coach speaks confidence-building truth and builds rapport with you. They will focus on the importance of discovery, curiosity and flexibility and have a positive attitude to change; they'll encourage you to focus on and enjoy every bit of your success.

Do these statements reflect what a spiritual searcher might find in a church in your locality?

Laurie Beth Jones, an American author has written a book called *Jesus, Life Coach*[35] which lays out a faith-based programme to help get our lives in shape, with Jesus as our personal trainer. The book suggests that we all want to be led by someone who will save us time, give us new ideas, connect with us on a personal level and stay with us on the journey, and Jesus promises all this and more. The questions at the end of each chapter offer the opportunity for any group to enjoy some stimulating discussion while looking at important principles for life, like focus, balance, productivity and fulfilment.

[35] Laurie Beth Jones, *Jesus, life coach* (Nashville: Thomas Nelson, 2004).

A look at the New Testament shows us that Jesus was the master life coach. People flocked to him. He constantly affirmed them, adjusted to them and inspired them. His coming to earth was the greatest single act of rapport-building in the world. We can't read the Great Commission without realising that Jesus gave people clear goals, a map to follow with himself beside. It's ironic that Jesus often comes up in secular life-coaching as a model to follow.

## get everything done and still have time to play

*Get everything done and still have time to play* is the title of a book by Mark Forster[36], a life coach who until recently, was the resources officer for the diocese of Chichester. This is a helpful book for anyone to read, with action questions at the end of each chapter, which could result in some interesting discussion in a group. Probably the most useful section of the book is the chapter on 'Learning to say No', which includes a helpful list of techniques

1. **Always use a neutral tone of voice when saying 'no' – never sound annoyed, shamefaced or harassed.**

2. **Be prepared to repeat your 'no' at least once.**

3. **Never give an excuse – if you do you will find yourself having to defend it.**

4. **Say something on the lines of 'I appreciate your asking me, but I can't fit that into my priorities at the moment.' Don't elaborate. If challenged, repeat it in the same neutral tone of voice. It's all right to give a reason such as 'I am concentrating right now on getting our new project**

completed.' **The more general the reason is, the less easy it is for someone to shoot it down.**

5. **If it's your boss doing the asking, try 'I can't fit that into the work priorities I have at the moment. Is there something you'd like me to put on hold for the moment so I can fit this in?' Again don't forget the neutral tone of voice!**

6. **If after saying 'no' you change your mind and decide you'd really like to do it after all, that's great! The point is that you are doing it because you want to and not because you feel you ought to.**

Some busy Christians might find these techniques useful as they decide to take on fewer church responsibilities in order to give more time to build up relationships with those within their circle of influence.

## story-telling

Everyone loves a story. 'The most fun weekend I've had in ages' was one woman's description of the two-day story-telling course she attended, according to an article in one of the popular women's magazines. 'You go to play, to tell stories, to analyse what they mean and why they're interesting.' On her course the mix was half male, half female with most in their thirties and forties and lively!

It seems that the ancient art of story-telling has been enjoying a revival in recent years. Story-telling is the ancient, 'let's sit around the fireside' tradition of stories you tell by heart while your audience looks you in the eye, and a browse on the Internet will

---

[36] Mark Forster, *Get everything done and still have time to play* (London: Hodder & Stoughton 2000).

# Jesus was a master story-teller... we need to learn from him how to communicate effectively and speak into people's lives convincingly

reveal a world of story-telling in Britain; schools, libraries and hospitals all use story-tellers. Why not launch a story-telling group in your community?

One group in Scotland did just that, aimed particularly at children in the school holidays. Carol writes

When I was growing up it was still common for extended families to live close together. Children could spend time with parents, grandparents, aunts and uncles and hear all manner of stories, many told without books. I recall learning many of the classic fairy stories; fantasies that included my favourite toys, animals and people; basic Bible stories and characters and my family's history in this way. It appeared to me that telling stories from memory, from the heart like this, seemed to come so naturally to that generation. Now, as life gets busier and more frantic for all of us, it's not easy for many parents to find the time, let alone the inclination or inspiration to fulfil this role. So we decided to hold a story-telling event – something traditional and relaxing – bringing together a few of the most harassed members of the community to experience quality time with family and friends.We put up posters and contacted friends to ask their support.

Having received little response from our adverts we were thrilled as the room started to fill with children and their mums or minders. Our story-teller, Grace, immediately put them at ease and the children and adults were spellbound, relaxed and happy as Grace gently and thoughtfully carried us through the Creation story layer by layer, using balloons, fabrics, stuffed animals and other carefully chosen props.

All too soon time came to share in refreshments and chat. As we said our goodbyes, the reluctance of our guests to leave assured us we had made new friends and opened a fresh door to some people.

So why not try it yourself. Log on to the Society for Storytelling website – www.sfs.org.uk for some ideas on how to get started.

Jesus was a master story-teller with a perfect knack for getting his message across by using all surrounding things to illustrate his point. We rather miss the point when we rattle on to twenty-first century urban congregations about shepherds and vineyards. We need to learn from him how to communicate effectively and speak into people's lives convincingly.

What kind of story is the gospel anyway? We'll give you a clue. Watch *Star Wars* or *Indiana Jones* or any similar film and you will recognise the 'Twelve Steps of the Hero's Journey' in a typical adventure story. A narrative analyst called Volger noticed recurring themes which he identified as twelve spheres of action in the hero's journey.

1. Ordinary world.
2. Call to adventure.
3. Refusal of the call.
4. Meeting the mentor (with whom you discover who you really are).
5. Crossing the first threshold.
6. Test allies and enemies.
7. The approach to the inmost cave.
8. Supreme ordeal.
9. Reward (seizing the sword).
10. The road back.
11. Resurrection (symbolic rebirth).
12. Return with the elixir.

Check it out with the gospel and if you think Jesus didn't initially refuse the call read the first few verses of John 2. What have you discovered about Jesus through this way of thinking outside the box?

In his book *Faith in a changing culture*, John Drane[37] outlines the importance of story-telling, suggesting that we use three kinds of stories. First of all, God's story. He's active and present in our world and we should tell these stories about him. As the book says

> The Bible unhesitatingly affirms that God is constantly at work in the world in many ways, times and places. Evangelism is not about Christians working on God's behalf because God is powerless without them. Effective evangelism must start with recognising where God is already at work, and getting alongside God in what is going on there. God's story, not ours, is the authentic starting point.

Secondly, Bible stories. Start wherever is appropriate for your listeners and fill in the detail later, but do it justice and bring it up to date. Then thirdly, Drane suggests we tell our own personal stories on the basis of 1 Peter 3:15, '... be prepared to give an answer... for the hope that you have'. So, let's go out and tell the greatest story ever told.

[37] John Drane, *Faith in a changing culture* (London: Marshall Pickering, 1997).

# the garden

## barbecues and picnics

Summer is traditionally time for barbecues – lots of sizzling sausages and burgers. But perhaps it's time for a new, healthy approach. There have been many articles warning us of obesity in the press recently. Remember the Galloping Gourmet? He's now a Christian, as well as a passionate advocate for healthy eating. He says this, 'How many people died on 9/11? I think it was 2,843. In the US this year one hundred times that number will die from overeating. The UK is behind but on a similar curve.'

So whilst eating out will always be a popular pastime, why not offer your neighbours and friends a healthier option – less food but better quality. Barbecue good lean meat with lightweight sauces, lots of salad and baked potatoes. Advertise it as being 'good for the heart.' Perhaps even use it as a fund-raiser to send money to a heart disease charity.

## bonfire party

I have fond childhood memories of the towering pyre on the waste ground on the corner, on which everyone piled the rubbish from their attic. Then, as the flames began to lick around Mrs Higginson's old settee, the acrid smoke would sting our eyes and cause everyone to scatter into the shadows. Sparks might well fly if you attempted this now: certainly environmental health would be affected.

But there's something about a fire that draws people to gather. Why not gather a group yourself? If you can't manage a mini bonfire you could invest in a chiminea from the garden centre and have a mini log fire in the garden.

Appease traditionalists with some home-made treacle toffee, baked potatoes, mulled wine and 'lashings of ginger beer'. People often feel far more involved in an event if they can contribute to it in some way. Suggest each person or family brings a box of fireworks (cost to be agreed beforehand) and something towards the food. There's no need to go overboard with fireworks and please do ensure local health and safety regulations are adhered to.

If you're really brave you could give all the little ones a sparkler and get them to write their name in the air. Then tell them (loud enough for their parents to hear) that Jesus already knows their name – he has it written on his heart. Pray for a starry night

and you'll have even more opportunity to point out the glory of God. 'The heavens declare the glory of God; the skies proclaim the work of his hands' (Ps. 19:1).

Events like this prior to Christmas may make it easier to invite people to something special at Christmas at which they'll have the opportunity to hear about the real reason for the season.

## days out with a difference

Jane was brought up in isolation in the wilds of West Wales and became aware of God through what he has made. She learnt to read God's presence in the wide-open sky, majestic cliffs and the loneliness of the desolate warrens. She wondered how tired, stressed out twenty-first people would react to being made aware of the wonder of God's creation.

Jesus used the physical world as a starting point for some of his teaching and used birds, flowers and the sky as visual aids (Lk. 12:7,27,54), so why not do the same? Jane organised a day consisting of a waterfall walk and a meal in a local hotel followed by an illustrated talk, along the lines of the special interest events advertised in the 'What's on this weekend' newspaper columns.

If you feel that you want to do some events specifically geared for men then find out the interests of the men you want to include and think about taking some risks. In his excellent book

*Wild at heart*, John Eldredge[38] says, 'Most messages for men ultimately fail. The reason is simple: They ignore what is deep and true to a man's heart, his real passions and try to shape him up through various forms of pressure. I offer this book, not as the seven steps to being a better Christian, but as a safari of the heart to recover a life of freedom, passion and adventure.' Eldredge speaks of the mighty men of the Bible going off into the wilderness to find God and themselves and how men's childhood dreams of battles and adventure and winning the beauty have been sadly tamed.

The growth in popularity of Experience Boxes in the larger department stores (where the gift is actually a voucher for a balloon ride, a 4x4 driving day or the opportunity to go white water rafting) and the growing trend for people to get sponsors and go off to walk the Great Wall of China, or some other such adventure, might also give us a strong clue to the desires of a man's heart.

Look at the type of action films enjoyed by men. Though some might be content with multiple armchair adventures, there is little doubt that some men are thirsting for something real, that will pump adrenaline round their veins. The Walk of a Thousand Men is one offer, but this annual event might not be enough and people who currently don't come to church can be excused for assuming that the most stimulating thing we have to offer a man is an occasional scramble up the church ladder to alter the steeple clock.

Evan is a part-time curate in Manchester and he also has a Christian media company called Fishfoodmedia. He feels that the traditional church experience can be a passive one for men and observed that those churches with more available activity seem to have a better male to female ratio. He recently celebrated his thirtieth birthday and a large group joined him on a paint-balling experience day. The men spent the day charging around woodland, ducking into thickets and firing paint pellets. They were exhausted but inexplicably happy. John Eldredge would have definitely approved.

So why not get a group of men together and go off on an adventure? It could be a paint-balling day, a hot-air balloon ride, clay pigeon shooting, sailing, a 4-wheel drive rally or simply a challenging hike. If you can spend the weekend away there will be more time for relaxing and chatting together, and if money is tight, then camping can be fun.

For a more passive experience take a group to the races, arrange snooker or bowling tournaments or get together in front of a big screen to watch a sporting event. The ever-popular WWE Wrestling events are great for pure showmanship and clean entertainment. The fights are choreographed but incredibly skilful.

And finally, don't forget the old adage that the way to a man's heart is through his stomach. Good food served as a breakfast or as an evening dinner is always popular and you might feel that those occasions are tailor-made to engage a speaker. But make

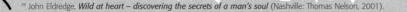

[38] John Eldredge, *Wild at heart – discovering the secrets of a man's soul* (Nashville: Thomas Nelson, 2001).

sure you have a good communicator or it might feel like another day in the boardroom and, at all costs, make sure that the speaker doesn't tell the men what they ought to be doing.

## garden parties/open gardens

Can you consider organising an event based on gardening hints – such as a local Gardener's World, or arrange a hanging basket demonstration? This could be held to your local garden centre if you don't feel you can do it yourself.

If your garden is a large one you might consider opening it to the public. Alternatively a group of people with more modest gardens can plan a tour. Be ready to answer questions about plants and flowers. You might be able to sell seeds and cuttings or arrange plant swaps. Take a look at www.quietgarden.co.uk for other ways of using your garden.

## camping

One group wanted to concentrate on building strong links with whole families and camping seemed a good way to include everyone. Camp was set up in the large garden of one home by the mums and children and the local Guides lent their dining and loo tents. Everyone arrived by 6.30 p.m. for a barbeque and communal games followed. A walk through local fields and woods began at 8 p.m. and the torchlight gave it all a magical feel. Hot chocolate and singing and stories around a bonfire followed before the children fell into their beds exhausted. The adults returned to the fire and the men particularly started to get to know each other

and to have some 'real' conversations. In the morning cereal and bacon butties were served for breakfast, and then more games before camp was packed up by midday.

The event was followed with regular get togethers for Sunday lunch and walks, and everyone is keen to repeat the camp next summer, but it will probably be twice the size. The secret of its success was the prayer for individuals beforehand.

## bouncy castles

If you thought Bouncy castles were just for children, think again. Some hire companies are now renting them to adults and throwing in some boxing gloves. Great for parties and an opportunity to prove that Christians are not wimps! Ring around the hire companies in your area for competitive prices. Some firms provide blow-up clubs to batter your opponent off *Gladiator*-style pedestals. Fun for all ages, and great for breaking the ice in your community. It could add a new dimension to a traditional barbeque.

## outdoor films

An outdoor film night can be a great success, though you'll need to wait until dusk for the picture to be clear enough. You can project the film onto your house wall or a screen. Make sure everyone brings a comfortable chair and is equipped for a drop in temperature. Use Citronella candles to deter midges and pass around crisps and popcorn.

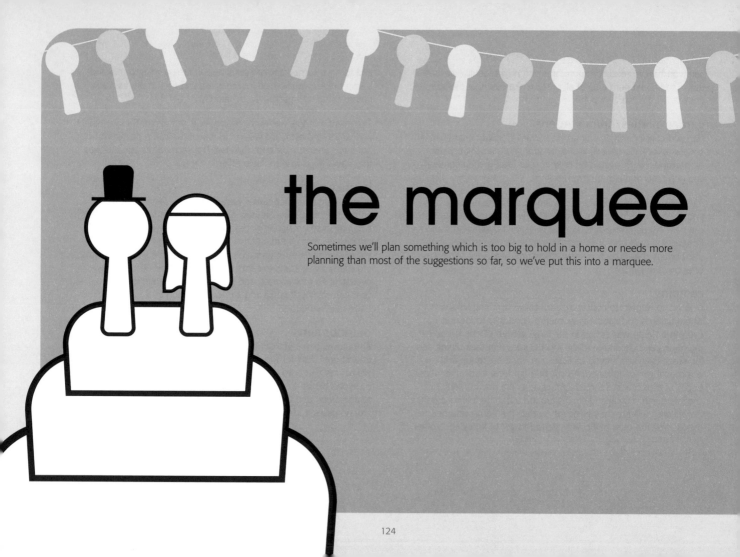

# the marquee

Sometimes we'll plan something which is too big to hold in a home or needs more planning than most of the suggestions so far, so we've put this into a marquee.

## international evening

'What are we going to do next?' was the question on the lips of the group responsible for co-ordinating events at a north-west London church. Sue reports on the answer.

One look at the one hundred plus congregation, consisting of people from approximately twenty-five to thirty different countries and we had the answer, an International Evening! What better way to celebrate the diversity of our environment than to offer the opportunity to invite their friends, family and colleagues to a fun evening. We publicised the evening using brightly coloured invitation cards decorated with flags and awaited the arrival of the guests, many wearing their national costume or international clothes they have acquired at some point, but never had the opportunity to wear! By prior arrangement, they brought some of the most delicious food you have ever tasted – yes, it really is curried goat over there!

On arrival everyone was given a glass of fruit punch and encouraged to take part in an icebreaker quiz, such as identifying famous places or famous international personalities from photos placed around the room. Later everyone moved into the main hall, colourfully decorated with flags and memorabilia from all over the world, where the food was labelled and arranged in various areas, representing different

corners of the world e.g. African, and Asian/Chinese dishes, West Indian main courses, European salads, and American desserts. Lots of informal recipe swapping ensued, as people tucked in and told each other how they cooked their particular dish. We'd like to produce our own recipe book from this event, but that's for the future!

Following the meal, there's a short talk, and then guests can choose to go and watch a variety of demonstrations on offer, from Chinese, Russian and West Indian cooking, Indian sari dressing, African hair-braiding, African head wraps and tie-dyeing. These sessions have proved to be extremely interesting and entertaining. Coffee and mints are then served and people chat long into the evening with new friends.

the
summer
house

Unexpected encounters can often surprise us when we realise that God can use these as much as what we consider to be more significant conversations. The stories here are included to challenge and encourage you.

## sarah's story

Sarah says:

In our fellowship group we're trying out being accountable to each other for our day-to-day evangelism. My close friend Pam is in the group. She teaches in a college and there is just one other Christian – a vicar's wife – on the (highly intellectual) staff, so she was saying that her chances of witnessing at work were limited. We all prayed that God would give her an opportunity that week to share her faith in an appropriate way.

The following week we met together and Pam started to regale us with a story that had obviously 'ruffled her feathers'. The Glastonbury festival was imminent and one of her colleagues had brought in the programme containing a section on creating an altar. Some of the other teachers thought this was a great lark and so one by one they had brought items into college and made an altar in the staff room.

The altar was a tray with stones and a candle on it, and people began bringing random things in to put upon the altar. They all thought it was highly amusing. The vicar's wife was clearly offended by the incident and Pam was trying to steer clear of the whole thing.

We had prayed specifically for her witness at work the week before, but Pam hadn't felt that this particular situation presented an opening for her to chat about her faith. It struck me how easily we can all fail to recognise opportunities because people don't necessarily come and ask us about our faith in the way we are conditioned to expect.

Pam's work colleagues are now busy organising a retreat in a Buddhist centre. She doesn't want to join the retreat, but she has decided to organise a night out afterwards in order to create an opportunity to ask them about it and offer her own perspective.

## anne's story - a time to listen? *

When I got home the other night, in addition to all the junk mail, there was one of those aggrieved notes from the postman complaining that he'd slogged all the way up the lane with a parcel for me only to find that I wasn't in. This meant that I had to go down to the parcel collection outpost of the Post Office to collect my Amazon order. Sounds easy but it's not. The said PO outpost is situated on a large roundabout with no parking anywhere. People cut across two lanes of traffic, stick their cars on double yellow lines and sprint into the office hoping that a lorry does not mash their rear-ends into metal porridge and (worse), Helga, the traffic warden doesn't get them.

Helga – not her real name – is a redoubtable lady about four foot six inches tall and similarly wide. She cannot be reasoned with, argued with, wept in front of, cajoled or bought. The roundabout is her special territory, and if you park there, she will get you. But I happen to know something about Helga. She is a creature of habit.

*This story first appeared in *The Good News*. Used with Thanks.

At 11 o'clock she meets with another traffic warden and they sneak off for a cup of tea in a local café. For a brief period, it's open season on the roundabout.

So off I went. The only trouble was, about twenty other people had had the same idea. There were so many hazard-warning lights flashing, it looked like a major pile-up. I squeezed into a tiny tributary off the main roundabout and made a dash for the Post Office. There was a queue of agitated people; all keeping an uneasy eye on the window and hoping Helga would be deep in gossip, or tempted by another currant bun.

Parcels are staffed by Jim. If you can't argue with Helga, you definitely can't rush Jim. Jim takes his time. Eventually it was my turn. I was feeling uneasy, because in the distance out of the window, I could see Helga emerging from the town centre with her friend. Jim smiled. 'Identification, please,' he said, as if he'd never seen me before.

On this occasion, I gave him my Church House pass that has my name and picture on it. He studied it for a minute. 'Board of Mission…' he mused. 'Is that, like, to do with missionaries?' 'Yes,' I said, not wanting to start a complicated conversation. 'You know I was in the Merchant Navy?' 'Yes. You know I do, you've told me a hundred times.' 'Did I ever tell you I once rescued a missionary from death?' 'No.' And I don't care, just give me the parcel!

Jim tucked my parcel comfortably under his arm. The phone rang, but he ignored it. And he told me a story of how, years ago, captaining a large ship, he came across a missionary struggling in a dinghy, trying to get between islands and overwhelmed by weather.

Jim rescued the man and took him in, half dead from exposure, and gave him chicken soup, because he'd been told that it was the 'right thing to do'. He rescued the man's belongings and dried them out, including the Bibles and religious literature that he had been trying to bring to the people of the islands. He saved his life.

Jim's eyes had gone rather dreamy, and he was clutching my parcel harder than ever. I was vaguely aware of the restless shifting of the people behind me and wondered if I was being told this story to brighten up Jim's otherwise dull day. Suddenly, a few people gave up and ran for it. Helga was back but I was stuck. My heart sank, here I was about to get a ticket, all because I'd been too soft to stop a dotty old bloke from telling me some fantasy rescue story. I'd stopped listening. Jim gave me the parcel and I signed for it. But he had something else he wanted me to sign. I reached for it.

'No, look,' he said crossly. From somewhere under his counter, he'd taken out a very old piece of paper, battered and creased, with old-fashioned print that was barely legible. On it was the Lord's Prayer. He said quietly. 'He gave me that. And I keep it by me and I say it every day. Helps me get through, you know, in here.' He gave me a conspiratorial nod.

Helga came in and fixed me with a maniacal stare. 'Is that YOUR car?' she barked, pointing out of the window. 'Yes,' I said miserably. 'MOVE IT!' she bawled. I couldn't believe my luck.

Back at home, I reflected on the many layers that had come out of a little trip to the Parcel Collection Office. My Church House pass sparked it, who would have thought of that? That one word *what other Post Office counters, supermarket checkouts, bank desks and market stalls have people with stories to tell about what God has done in their life? How on earth do we create the space to hear them?*

'mission' had released the story of a powerful encounter in which it was a missionary who needed the help, compassion and care of others to do God's work. Without that chicken soup, God's messenger might not have survived. Out of that encounter came a message, a resource that sustained another in the years to come. And as for me, I nearly missed it. I was in a hurry and was concerned about my own selfish well-being. I didn't want to hear the story and because my own concerns were paramount I was ready to dismiss it. Another few seconds and I would never have known about the Lord's Prayer and its part in Jim's life. If I had got the ticket I might not have cared. All I wanted was to walk in, get the parcel, walk out, and go home. But if I call myself a 'missionary', why do I not ask where else the encounter presents itself? What other Post Office counters, supermarket checkouts, bank desks and market stalls have people with stories to tell about what God has done in their life? How on earth do we create the space to hear them? How shall we hear? Maybe, just maybe, Helga too has a story to tell, if not that, at least once, she allowed a motorist to get away with it. Why did this happen? If I go past the café at 11 o'clock, I am resolved to find out.

Sometimes we can prejudge people and assume they are not interested in faith issues and then find we are totally wrong in our judgement – which can be a humbling process. Here are two such encounters from Kerry and Elaine:

### kerry's story

Some long-standing musician friends came over to visit from Ireland. They wanted to see lots of friends and knew it wasn't possible to get around everyone, so Pete – another of their friends – set up a Sunday lunchtime music session in a pub quite near to where we live and we went to join in. We don't tend to go in pubs very often as we get caught up so much with church events. I'm sure there is a lesson to be learned there!

Anyway, the session was a great success and lots of people gathered to hear the songs. The atmosphere was really friendly and people joined in and sang along. The landlady of the pub – even brought drinks across to those who were leading the music.

I got chatting to Pete's girlfriend Marie and really liked her. During the course of the conversation I mentioned that we'd come straight from church and she seemed to ignore the comment totally and changed the subject, so I assumed she wasn't interested or might even be a bit hostile to Christianity.

The next time the Irish friends came over, Pete organised another session at the same pub, this time on the Sunday night and we went enthusiastically to join in. Marie had brought a neighbour along who'd been recently widowed and it turned out that our vicar had conducted the funeral and they'd really liked him.

Marie then started talking to me about her own father's death. The family had nursed him for a long time, yet she said she still felt guilty about things. 'For example – I regret that it didn't occur to me to say Night Prayers with him,' she told me, 'He always did them with us when we were little and I still say them regularly now. We ought to have done it together; I think it would have blessed him.'

'Oh,' I said, showing my surprise. 'I didn't realise you were a believer,' She assured me that she was and added that she'd been brought up as a Roman Catholic. We then talked about the importance of 'owning' the faith that you've been brought up with and I realised that she had indeed owned it. Though she wasn't part of a worshipping community, she talked to God when out riding or walking her dogs. It's just too easy to think that churchgoers have the monopoly on faith. I won't make that mistake again.

## aoife's story

Aoife's story begins just after the death of her husband, Mark and concerns a business colleague of his.

Sometimes I really don't just get it. The Bible clearly tells us not to judge yet I find myself in situations where I have already prejudged someone after just a few times of meeting them and chatting.

For example, Jim blew me away after Mark died. Thinking I had 'sussed' him out over the last eighteen years, I really believed that Jim had no faith in God at all. Over the years he has fallen out with several members of his own family, often not speaking to them for years. I know he loves his wife and children and would do absolutely anything for them but as far as anyone else goes, they really wouldn't want to cross him, though he has only ever shown me courtesy.

I spoke with Jim many times following Mark's death but I will never forget the very first time, just three days after. He asked me how I was coping and I said that because I knew where Mark was and because of my faith in God I was OK and peaceful. I then went on to say something like, 'I don't expect you to understand'. He then told me this story in front of his wife who had never heard it before. Whilst he was away from home, as a young child, recovering from rheumatic fever, he was lodged with a Christian family and was taught Scripture every day. He then went on to say that he prays every night before he goes to bed!

I was flabbergasted a few days later when, during a phone call, he talked more about this and he then went on to quote John 3:16 to me, 'For God so loved the world that he gave his one and only

Son, that whoever believes in him shall not perish but have eternal life'. I decided to use this scripture on the order of service for my husband's celebration service. I was extremely challenged by my judgemental attitude. Will I ever learn?

I have always got on well with my neighbour Andrea, yet we haven't really got to the 'come over and have coffee' stage, mainly because of work commitments and the fact that our children are different ages. I wanted to do some scrapbooking and this led to a session with the women in my church and Andrea came even though she only knew one other of my friends. Suddenly I have begun to see more of her and we have discovered a mutual interest in reading, so we are going to start a book club together. Andrea loaned me a series of books about a small village in America called Mitford. The books are known as the *Mitford Stories*.[39] What amazed me the most was, that they are full of Scripture, based on the life of Father Tim who is a pastor, and those around him. The characters face all sorts of hardships and Father Tim is there bringing God's love and prayers and an abundance of Scripture.

My neighbour does not go to church except for weddings and christenings yet she loves these books. If I had read them first I probably wouldn't have lent them to an 'unchurched' friend, yet they are fantastic stories of how God works in people's lives. This sharing of books and opinions has really opened up something in our conversations that was never there before. How dare I judge? We are all on a journey and what right have I to think I know where people are on theirs?

*how dare I judge?
we are all on a journey and
what right have I to think I know
where people are on theirs?*

[39] Jan Karon, *The Mitford Stories* (London: Penguin, 1996-2003).

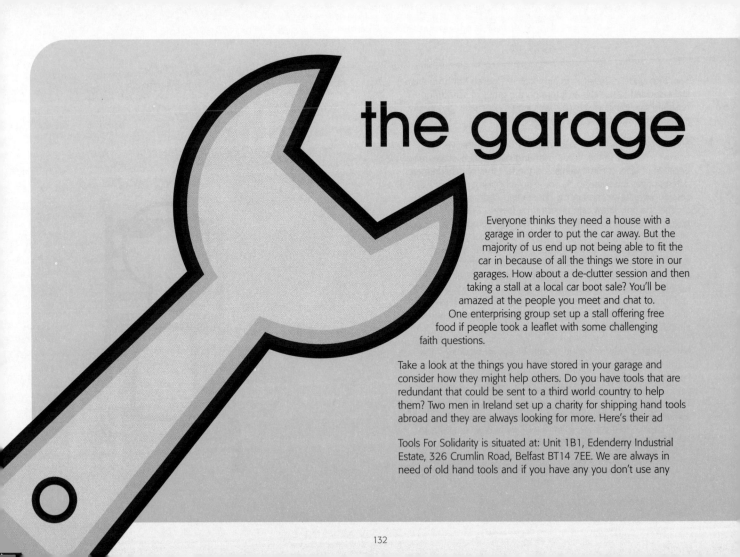

# the garage

Everyone thinks they need a house with a garage in order to put the car away. But the majority of us end up not being able to fit the car in because of all the things we store in our garages. How about a de-clutter session and then taking a stall at a local car boot sale? You'll be amazed at the people you meet and chat to. One enterprising group set up a stall offering free food if people took a leaflet with some challenging faith questions.

Take a look at the things you have stored in your garage and consider how they might help others. Do you have tools that are redundant that could be sent to a third world country to help them? Two men in Ireland set up a charity for shipping hand tools abroad and they are always looking for more. Here's their ad

Tools For Solidarity is situated at: Unit 1B1, Edenderry Industrial Estate, 326 Crumlin Road, Belfast BT14 7EE. We are always in need of old hand tools and if you have any you don't use any

*there are so many God-given opportunities to talk about our faith. We can't always expect to give the same three point message, sometimes people will approach us from random angles, and we just need to be able to identify a potential peg on which we can hang our message.*

more or would like to come and visit our groovy centre and get your hands dirty give us a ring on 028 90747473 or e-mail tools.belfast@virgin.net.

## shoeboxes

How many shoe boxes are you hanging onto just in case something goes wrong with the shoes and you need to return them? Can they be filled with gifts for an underprivileged child? Samaritan's Purse is one of several organisations that send lorry-loads of shoeboxes to war-torn countries every year. Operation Christmas Child brings joy and hope to children in desperate situations around the world through gift-filled shoeboxes and the good news of God's love. This programme provides an opportunity for people of all ages to be involved in a simple, hands-on mission project while focusing on the true meaning of Christmas, Jesus Christ, God's greatest gift. Along with shoebox gifts, millions of children are given gospel booklets in their own language. Samaritan's Purse collect over 6.6 million shoebox gifts worldwide and distribute them to children in some ninety-five countries.

Samaritan's Purse supply leaflets explaining the concept and suggesting what might be appropriate to go in the boxes (for example they ask you not to include war-toys or aerosols). Could you get together with the neighbours and put together a pile of gift-filled boxes? People often love to be involved in something which has a feel-good factor, especially if children benefit from their efforts. Once your shoebox is packed, you can drop it off at one of hundreds of locations around the nation. Contact Samaritan's Purse direct for further details: Samaritan's Purse International, Ltd. Victoria House, Victoria Road, Buckhurst Hill, Essex 1G9 5EX. Telephone: 020 8559 2044 Fax: 020 8502 9062

E-mail: uk@samaritan.org www.samaritanspurse.org

## cars

And finally, since we're in the garage, what about your car? When you have it serviced or have the tyres checked do you ever chat with the people doing it? At the very least you can leave a relevant leaflet in the car so that the mechanic can glance at it; it might just speak right into their life.

Our local garage is wonderful. Three brothers run it and they're very personable and chat about their families and they fall over themselves to give a brilliant service. One of my friends lives right near there. She called them out to start her car several times and they refused money but told her they liked chocolate biscuits. So I occasionally drop in with a box of biscuits and a card telling them how much I appreciate them (I do the same with the car spares shop who insist on fitting bulbs and wiper blades for me – I must have perfected the pathetic woman look!).

Perhaps I shouldn't admit this in print, but recently I forgot to book in for my MOT and realised with horror that it had expired a few weeks earlier. The garage fitted me in the same day. When I went to pick it up I commented on the Rogues Gallery page in our local press, which listed the sins of locals who have been in trouble. Some listings are for driving without documentation and I could well have featured among them! The mechanic grinned at me and said, 'God looks after his own.' So I told him that was true in so many ways and if he believed that, he'd better join God's gang straight away. Another time I went to get my tyres checked at another local supplier. He was looking for my toolkit and opened my boot, which is stacked high with evangelism resources. He turned and grinned at me and asked, 'Are you leaving home?' When I said this was work stuff he asked, 'Well what kind of a vicar are you?'

I told him I wanted to connect faith with modern culture and he asked me if anyone had ever talked to me about out of body experiences. With a bit of prompting he told me about his own experience of this phenomenon. He acknowledged that the essence, which was him, was able to exist separately from the shell, which is his body. I asked him if he was able to accept that when his body died this would be able to continue to exist and he agreed. So I asked him 'Where do you want it to go?' That was obviously a powerful question and he reacted, 'Wow, are you asking me do I want it to live in heaven or Hawaii?'

When I nodded he said he needed time to think about that one. So I told him that was fine but pointed out that only God knew him intimately and loved him unconditionally. Only God was able to heal his brokenness and made him whole and happy. I've left him to think about it. My customer details are on the computer and we've chatted about my church so he knows where to find me in an emergency. Otherwise I'm leaving it to God to prompt him to follow up the conversation next time I get my tyre treads checked.

There are so many God-given opportunities to talk about our faith. We can't always expect to give the same three point message, sometimes people will approach us from random angles, and we just need to be able to identify a potential peg on which we can hang our message.

# now is the time

'The important work of moving the world forward, does not wait to be done by perfect men and women.' George Eliot 1819-1880[40]

Hopefully some of the ideas in this book will have inspired you to consider ways of reaching into your community in creative ways. Now comes the need for action. Sometimes we can be fearful of doing something new or of being rejected if we begin to build relationships with new people. There is a danger of always feeling we need to wait until we've done this course, or been to that conference. We're always putting off actually getting involved and doing something. We need to understand that God isn't looking for perfection, but a willingness to 'go' into our communities and 'be' salt and light, just as we are.

Once we've built up a small group of friends who are interested in finding out more about our faith, we can have an expectation that they will follow the traditional route to church, and eventually join us in worship on Sunday and midweek. But it's important that we allow God to work in other people's lives in a different way to ours.

Some people will, because of their relationship with us, be happy to join us at church on a Sunday. However, it may that, because of family circumstances, work commitments or a variety of other reasons, some of our friends never become part of our local fellowship. For them church may be a small group which meets in a home on a Wednesday evening, or some other gathering of Christians which may look nothing like church to us.

For further reading on this, *The shaping of things to come* by Michael Frost and Alan Hirsch[41] is an excellent book. In his book, *A generous orthodoxy*, Brian McLaren[42] says, 'To be a Christian in the generous, orthodox way is to live and grow in a loving community of people who are seeking truth on the road of mission, and who have been launched on the quest by Jesus, who is with us, and guides us still.'

## one day you're looking back...

One of the saddest emotions in life must surely be regret. Often we can be sorry that we've done or not done a certain act – that's why we're so thrilled that God builds in a repentance and forgiveness clause into our relationship. To reach the latter days of your life and regret not being bolder in sharing faith with others, must be hard to live with.

We need to be bolder and not procrastinate, to initiate meaningful conversations instead of engaging in superficial ones. Hopefully this book will have given you some ideas of how you can create opportunities to get alongside people and provide forums for discussion in creative, non-threatening ways. If you don't feel you can risk sounding preachy then asking questions is a good way to do it. But do it now.

So often, we don't do it though, do we? We use that well-worn phrase 'I don't do'. Consider the following story from Leonard Sweet.

[40] *The Times Book of Quotations* (London: HarperCollins, 2000). [41] Michael Frost and Alan Hirsch, *The shaping of things to come* (USA Massachusetts and Australia Erina, NSW: Hendrickson Publishing, 2004). [42] Brian McLaren, *A generous orthodoxy* (Grand Rapids: Zondervan, 2004).

One of our students received an appointment from a bishop, and the student did not feel the placement exactly suited his abilities. I overheard him complaining about it to another student, and then the other student said, 'You know, the world's a better place because Michelangelo did not say, 'I don't do ceilings.' ' Her comment stopped me dead in my tracks. I had to admit she was right. If you and I are going to be faithful to the ministry God is calling us to, then we had better understand that. I reflected on the attitudes of key people throughout the Scriptures and the history of the church.

The world's a better place because a German monk named Martin Luther did not say, *'I don't do doors.'*
The world's a better place because an Oxford don named John Wesley didn't say *'I don't do preaching in fields.'*
The world's a better place because Moses didn't say, *'I don't do Pharaohs or mass migrations.'*
The world's a better place because Noah didn't say, *'I don't do arks and animals.'*
The world's a better place because Rahab didn't say, *'I don't do enemy spies.'*
The world's a better place because Ruth didn't say, *'I don't do mothers-in-law.'*
The world's a better place because Samuel didn't say, *'I don't do mornings.'*
The world's a better place because David didn't say, *'I don't do giants.'*
The world's a better place because Peter didn't say *'I don't do Gentiles.'*
The world's a better place because John didn't say, *'I don't do deserts.'*
The world's a better place because Mary didn't say, *'I don't do virgin births.'*
The world's a better place because Paul didn't say, *'I don't do correspondence.'*
The world's a better place because Mary Magdalene didn't say, *'I don't do feet.'*
The world's a better place because Jesus didn't say, *'I don't do crosses.'*

And the world will be a better place only if you and I don't say, *'I don't do...'*

'twenty years from now you'll be more disappointed by the things you didn't do, than by the ones you did.

so throw off the bowlines, sail away from the safe harbour, catch the trade winds in your sails.
explore. dream. discover.'

**MARK TWAIN**

# references

Peter Drucker, *Managing for the future – the 1990s and beyond* (Middlesex: Penguin, 1992).

The bridge photo appeared in the *National Geographic* magazine in November 1999. Taken by Vincent Musi.

George Lings, *Encounters on the Edge – living proof – a new way of being church?* (The Sheffield Centre, 1999).

David Coffey, Address to the Baptist Assembly, 2002.

John Young, *Christian Herald*.

Ed Silvoso, *Prayer Evangelism* (California: Regal, 2000).

Melanie Phillips, *The Sex Change Society* (The Social Market Foundation, 1999).

Taken from Nick Pollard's *'Gender Roles'* article, first published in *Idea* magazine. Used by permission. See www.culturewatch.org.

Poll analysis by Jim Mann, *Observer Research Department*.

Poem by Phyllis Hill published in: Lever and Lochhead, (eds.), *West in her eye: Poems by women* (Pyramid Press, 1995).

Social Trends – National statistics, Census 2001.

Eugene H. Peterson, *The Message* (Colorado: Navpress, 2002).

*The Times Book of Quotations* (London: HarperCollins, 2000).

National statistics, Census 2001.

*The Times Book of Quotations* (London: HarperCollins, 2000).

Louis Sachar, *Holes* (Collins Educational, 2001).

*The Female Lifestyle Survey of Great Britain*, commissioned by *Top Sante* magazine, the most comprehensive survey of women's attitudes towards their lives and work ever carried out.

*The Times Book of Quotations* (London: HarperCollins, 2000).

Laurie Beth Jones, *Jesus CEO* (New York: Hyperion, 1995).

*The Times Book of Quotations* (London: HarperCollins, 2000).

Marcus Buckingham and Donald O. Clifton, *Now Discover your strengths* (London: Simon & Schuster, 2001).

*The Times Book of Quotations* (London: HarperCollins, 2000).

*The Times Book of Quotations* (London: HarperCollins, 2000).

Jack Dominian, *Let's make love* (Darton, Longman and Todd, 2001).

Paulo Coelho, *Eleven Minutes* (London: HarperCollins, 2003).
See also Eve Ensler, *The Vagina Monologues*,(London: Virago, 2001).

*The Times Book of Quotations* (London: HarperCollins, 2000).

Pablo Martinez and Ali Hull, *Tracing the Rainbow* (Carlisle: Spring Harvest Publishing Division/Authentic Media, 2004).

*Evangelicals Now*, May 2003.

*The Times Book of Quotations* (London: HarperCollins, 2000).

*The Times Book of Quotations* (London: HarperCollins, 2000).

*The Times Book of Quotations* (London: HarperCollins, 2000).

*The Times Book of Quotations* (London: HarperCollins, 2000).

*The Times Book of Quotations* (London: HarperCollins, 2000).

Laurie Beth Jones, *Jesus, life coach* (Nashville: Thomas Nelson, 2004).

Mark Forster, *Get everything done and still have time to play* (London: Hodder & Stoughton 2000).

John Drane, *Faith in a changing culture* (London: Marshall Pickering, 1997).

John Eldredge, *Wild at heart – discovering the secrets of a man's soul* (Nashville: Thomas Nelson, 2001).

Jan Karon, *The Mitford Stories* (London: Penguin, 1996-2003).

*The Times Book of Quotations* (London: HarperCollins, 2000).

Michael Frost and Alan Hirsch, *The shaping of things to come* (USA Massachusetts and Australia Erina, NSW: Hendrickson Publishing, 2004).

Brian McLaren, *A generous orthodoxy* (Grand Rapids: Zondervan, 2004).

entered into? There are many recent descriptions of this worthy of fuller attention, which include Factor and Pitts (2001) and McKee et al (2010).

In providing its full response to the government's Green Paper, *Youth matters* (DfES, 2005), CYWU held a seminar to produce a response, and in the first section gave useful definitions of the Youth Service and youth work as follows:

> By Youth Service CYWU means the partnership between Local Authorities and voluntary organisations which has as its prime purpose the provision of support, social, personal and developmental education to young people between the ages of 13 and 25 provided by trained and JNC qualified youth and community workers, working full or part time and with or without the assistance of trained and supported volunteers. It is a unique service that begins and ends with the needs of young people and takes their support as its guiding principle on the value base, methodology and purpose expressed in *Transforming youth work: Resourcing excellent youth services.*

> By youth work CYWU means those practices which exist within the Youth Service as defined above which are developed by JNC qualified youth workers and those under their direction. It is an informal educational intervention in the whole life of a young person that depends upon a voluntary choice by the young person to become involved. It offers a process of personal and social development. This process seeks to empower the young person and fulfil their emotional, intellectual and social capacities through experiences and reflection on them. It offers young people new activities and ideas and helps them become aware of the virtues of respect, tolerance, community and civic life. It seeks to create greater understanding of rights and responsibilities and

—

39

to support the needs of young people themselves as active citizens with entitlements and a social role to play. It encourages participation, and challenges those ideas and behaviours deemed anti social and divisive. (CYWU, 2005, p 2)

## An empowering profession

Youth work as defined here seeks to tip the balance of power in young people's favour – young people are perceived and received within it as young people. The method starts where young people who present themselves to the service actually start themselves. Its focus is on the young person as an individual and it is responsive to peer processes and groups and wider networks and cultural and social identities. It is concerned with how young people feel as well as with what they know and can do. Its effects can be very quickly transformative or, longer term, significant, but less noticeable than other measurable outputs.

This practice represents a significant advance within the spectrum of educational interventions and a combination of methods in accessible settings that are particularly conducive to the modern policy and social context. Far from being a remedial club-based method it is an elaborate and sensitive practice uniquely placed to advance young people and their issues.

Youth work skills are deployed in a wide variety of settings, from street-based detached work to centre-based and issue work, to mobile units and international exchanges. The media involved range from music to sports, to play and discussion and democratic political participation. That the youth work method be central must be the main purpose of the provision, whether in uniformed, faith-based, sporting, housing or other more generic organisations.

Descriptions of the method of youth work in its social and educational contexts are numerous and sophisticated, and recent works worthy of attention are listed in the 'References and further reading' section under Batsleer (2008), Brent (2009), Davies (2005),

Factor and Pitts (2001), Jeffs and Smith (2005), Sapin (2009), Sercombe (2010), Williamson (1995) and Young (2006). What I have emphasised in this opening chapter is how what is done is grounded in ethical values which are collectivised and expressed in the context of rights and social purposes. Youth work does not exist in an anarchic alternative sphere withdrawn from the sordid world around it. It has sought to change that world and transform the policies of the state and the media towards young people. Because of the engagement of youth work practitioners in key state formulations of the work there is the potential for a policy framework that is progressive and challenging of the predominant neoliberal order. But to achieve this, the profession itself must be empowered (McConnell, 1996).

England was the first country to plot its demolition. The full signature of this struggle to demolish and resist can best be analysed by considering the evidence submitted to the Parliamentary Education Select Committee on young people's services in 2010/11 and then the consultative documents submitted to the government consultation exercise 'Positive for Youth' in 2011 and their subsequent policy document of the same title. CYWU/Unite's extensive and comprehensive submission to this consultative exercise provides one of the key points in the contemporary definition of purpose and place of youth work. Relevant documents are listed in the 'References and further reading' section (see House of Commons Education Committee, 2011a, 2011b, 2011c, 2011d, 2012; DfE, 2011a, 2011b, 2011c, 2011d, 2011e; Unite, 2011).

What emerged from this very significant struggle was of substantial importance. Youth work's role as an educational, distinct professional practice was preserved, alongside a recognition that it was best delivered on young people's terms through 'open access' provision, that is, services which depend on the voluntary engagement of young people. A government-led assault on these underpinning virtues, which had its origin in the early 1980s Thatcherite rejection of the Thompson Report (DfES, 1982) and subsequent attempts to introduce an anaesthetised 'curriculum' (Ministerial Conferences Steering Committee, 1990) was, in effect, blunted and substantially

—

slowed down. Bearing in mind that all such matters are relative, the outcome could have been a lot worse, and the fact that it wasn't was largely due to the young people and youth workers in the Choose Youth campaign.

## Summary

Youth work is vitally important within society's commitment to lifelong learning, inclusion and democracy. It is where informal learning takes place. From the voluntary relationship established with young people a dialogue begins that develops through trust and mutuality into professional friendship and a form of educative and supportive accompaniment. In such a relationship the rights and voices of young people are primary. Youth workers have built a unique public service out of this relationship and it has always been difficult for the state to contain this approach in its wider endeavours to manage the market economy, creating youth unemployment and the necessary demonisation of young people.

Youth work has therefore offered an alternative human vision of the economy. It offers a vision of an economy with human beings at the centre which is greatly significant and much more than a form of benign philanthropy, or a soft sentiment. It is a glimpse today and at a micro level of what could be the possibilities tomorrow globally. Youth work signals the creation of a world of individual human potentialities authentically realised in new forms of social relationships. Just as a nationalised health service free at the point of need or a free education system from cradle to grave signal an advance in civilisation and social cooperation, so youth work represents an advance in social and educational commitments and practice.

Youth work has extended the scope of education beyond the classroom and into life. Importantly for current concerns, it has extended the prospect of education into the development of consciousness and political action.

These lofty descriptions and aspirations do not always fit with the suppressive restrictions on practice experienced every day. But